Good News People in Action

William F. Keucher

JUDSON PRESS • VALLEY FORGE

GOOD NEWS PEOPLE IN ACTION

Translations of the Bible quoted in this book are as follows:

The Holy Bible, the Revised Standard Version of the Bible, © copyright 1946 and 1952 by the Division of Christian Education of the National Council of the Churches of Christ in the United States of America. Used by permission.

The Holy Bible, King James Version.

The Living Bible. Copyright © 1971 by Tyndale House Publishers, Wheaton, Illinois. Used by permission.

The Bible: A New Translation by James Moffatt. Copyright 1954 by James Moffatt. By permission of Harper & Row, Publishers, Inc.

The New English Bible. © The Delegates of the Oxford University Press and The Syndics of the Cambridge University Press 1961, 1970. Reprinted by permission.

Good News for Modern Man, Today's English Version. Copyright © American Bible Society, 1966.

Library of Congress Cataloging in Publication Data

Keucher, William F.
    Good news people in action.

    Includes bibliographical references.
    1. Evangelistic work.   2. Witness bearing (Christianity) I. Title.
BV3790.K493   269'.2   74-30039
ISBN 0-8170-0671-0

Printed in the U.S.A. ⊕

Photographs on pages 9, 17, 31, and 60 are by H. Armstrong Roberts; on pages 25 and 75 by Wallowitch; on pages 42, 50, and 65 by Clark and Clark; and on page 82 by Gunter Wall.

Contents

Foreword   5

Introduction   7

1   Exchanging Bad News for Good News   9

2   Good News—Promise and Event   17

3   Good News for Everyone, Everywhere   25

4   Good News for the Whole Person   31

5   Picturing the New Person in Christ   37

6   The Evangelistic Life Style of Good News People   45

7   Models for a Person-to-Person Witness   55

8   Good News—Where We Live   65

9   Deciding for the Good News   73

10 The Good News in Action   81

Epilogue   91

Appendixes

   A. "Leading" in Person-to-Person Witnessing   93

   B. A Checklist on Effective Attitudes

      in Creating a Helping Relationship   95

To the people of
The Covenant Baptist Church
whose love
helped to write this book

Foreword

Dr. Keucher was asked to assume the role of a "tractarian" to awaken from spiritual lethargy, release and liberate dumb mouths, and embolden timid spirits to bear witness to Jesus Christ in order that the miracle of conversion might occur in many lives.

In this day, when to be free from internal restraints and external constraints has become a cultic obsession and when expression and exposure of our being is regarded as the style of health and wholeness, a mysterious inhibition locks us into silent repression of "the Name which is above every name. . . ."

Could it be that the human spirit which finally names the name of Jesus as the center of being and circumference of existence has touched eternity in time and the meaning of human wholeness? To confess we love Jesus and to entreat others to love him entails crucifixion, death to pride, nailing it on the cross of offense, before we observe the miracle of new creation, life born anew to a life of hope, a reenactment of the third day.

The central burden of *Good News People in Action* is the unique particularity of an "evangelistic life style" people; the depth and breadth and height of history and tradition and meaning out of which they finally name the name of Jesus; and what the name embraces and gathers up in a totality—past, present, and future, history and beyond history, persons and "principalities and powers," time and eternity, this world and the world to come. Naming the name of Jesus to another human soul; the event of a personal conversion; God's eternal incessant mission of making "all things new"; the final chapter of "a new heaven and a new earth" are all of one piece in Dr. Keucher's treatment of an "evangelistic life style."

The writer was asked to deal with the subject of personal witnessing, simply. There is no simple way, because the Good News is profound, impenetrably profound; and the illusions of simplicity are stripped and we are plunged into the depths. The writer was asked to focus on practical ways and methods of witnessing, but he has made it clear that the smallest acts and deeds must be linked to the whole cosmos of God's eternal activity and purpose, just as a single flower is sustained by the complexity of the whole universe, and the conversion and renewal of one life is cradled in God's total creative and redemptive history, so that the antecedent millenniums of time and creation and the future eternities of hope and consummation are all essential realities to provide meaning to a single life, to a human community, or to a nation.

Dr. Keucher has brought to this creative task his enormous capabilities and gifts born out of his roles as denominational executive, pastor and preacher, and an ever-growing mind and spirit as a theologian whose central task is to interpret reality in the light of ultimate reality.

Jitsuo Morikawa
Associate Executive Secretary
American Baptist National Ministries
Valley Forge, Pennsylvania

Introduction

A pastor tells of watching the inner harbor in Cleveland. It was still frozen over and clogged with ice floes. A huge icebreaker was battering its way, seeking to make a channel for one of the first ships to leave the harbor for the open lake. After the icebreaker and then the freighter had slipped away, he was left in silence. But in the stillness of that morning and in the warmth of the sun, he began to hear what he described as "a number of rustling garments" or "fairy bells." It dawned on him that he was listening to the melting of thousands of tiny ice crystals beneath the rays of the morning sun. The sound was more beautiful than prayer, like the sound of the Holy Spirit passing by. A week later when he returned, the ice was gone and the waters of the lake flowed blue from shore to outer horizon. A miracle of God had taken place, for the sun had accomplished and completed what all the power of large machinery could not do. In much the same way God's love can melt the frozen waste of unconcern in us. We are awakening to our personal needs and to the resources beyond ourselves. In the promise and the power of God's own Spirit, clogged channels in the life of the church can flow again and God's people can be enabled to be Good News people engaged in person-to-person witness.

W.F.K.

1 | Exchanging Bad News for Good News

In the beginning, the news was so good! Out of chaos, God's world in order stood. Bright colors of the prism's shining hood he planted in the foliage of the woods and in the flowers flaming everywhere. Then, draped around the waist of dancing earth, God tied a rainbow sash of slender girth. A yellow moon awakened harvest mirth, as cosmos praised its Maker for its worth. God blessed his world, when, like the stars in space, he traced each planet's race in its own place. Then, when the aeon's time had run its course, God looked upon creation and endorsed its nature and its purpose; where, as planned, each part was held together in his hand. From dusk to dawn, when earth has

gone to bed, until next sunset paints the sky in red, the beauty of the earth reflects its head. "Behold! It all is very good," he said. Who could have known how men would rape God's earth; in guilt, conceive their Babels for hard births!

These lines suggest the paradox of our creation, together with the dilemmas which we face as members of the human family. God made all things bright and beautiful, even as he made man—"male and female he created them"—in his own image and likeness. But, if God made a good beginning, we have spoiled it all by sinning. There is beauty, but it is disfigured with sordid ugliness of human origin. There is order in the world, but it is mixed with the disorder of our selfish plundering which upsets the delicate balance of nature's ways. There is harmony in the world, but raucous voices spoil creation's song. There is goodness everywhere, but we mix this goodness of the world with our own evil to make a witch's cauldron of destructive brew. There is love, but we prostitute our own affections and those of others to justify ourselves and to buy what God intends should belong to us as a free gift. There is hope, but its presence only serves to deepen the despair of our existence. There is faith, but we distort its functions into rigid forms and systems designed to let us hide from the call of God, the claim of our neighbor, and from honest self-awareness. There is life, but we have lost its savor and its flavor. The life we seek to lead outside of God is filled with dread and is a living death. Our bodies, destined as a dwelling place for the Most High God, experience his presence as wrath and torment, if not as God-forsakenness and emptiness. *The paradox is* that God made the world good, but we, who were assigned a trust as stewards, have proved false to that trust and have remade the world evil, reflecting the distorted features of our own faithless existence. *The paradox is* that God made the earth as a temple to be filled with his presence and to declare his glory and to show forth his faithfulness until the end of time, but we have defaced the temple, defiled and desecrated the presence and debased its meaning for our human existence. *The paradox is* that God made the world of nature as a living system of delicate balance and interdependence, but we have upset the balance by denuding fields of trees, plowing up the precious prairie sod which served as a watershed, while using up the nutriments of soil and squandering the resources in the air and in the ground, as though our generation were to be the last. *The paradox is* that God made fresh air to breathe and pure streams to flow to quench our thirst and cleanse the stain of living, but our smog pollutes the air we breathe and our untreated waste despoils our streams. *The paradox is* that God made us to be his partners in building up the earth and in nurturing the entire human family to share in its goodness and its plenty, but we have dissolved our partnership and have been busy tearing down the earth which is our common home, while building walls and fences to shut out our neighbors. *The paradox is* that God has afforded us a creative freedom for our task to live with integrity and wholeness, enjoying the gifts of his hands and the fruits of our labors; but we have become a civil war within ourselves. We are alienated from ourselves, as well as from our family, and alienated from the world of nature. Our alienation is our human bondage. Hell is not only other people; we, ourselves, are hell, with all its torment—and from this hell we find no exit.

The paradox is—in short—that we, created by God as sons and daughters, are sinners and defectors. Created by God to know one life, we are legion, whose lives are no longer whole, but broken and scattered among our many divided selves, each one clamoring for recognition. With integrity gone, we have suffered a loss of sure identity.

The paradox is that we, created by God to live in the human family because he saw it was not good for man to live alone, like Cain, have killed our brother. We carry the mark of Cain wherever we traverse the earth; being guilty of spiritual regicide whereby we prove disloyal to Christ's lordship, we find it easier to practice fratricide. Meant by God to live interdependently in our partnership with him and with others as our brothers and sisters, and with nature as the transcript of our ecological existence, we have lapsed into a false autonomy. We find ourselves living out of our own meager resources of impoverished inner being, instead of living out of God's fullness. We live independently of those whom God has given us to love and serve, and in the midst of a crowd we suffer anguished loneliness in its awful intensity, more than Admiral Byrd knew in Antarctica. Lacking love, we cannot give its legal tender, which is justice; and lacking both love and justice, we cannot experience mercy for ourselves. Without mercy to temper our hostility, anger, and aggression, we act destructively to destroy our neighbor and our world and, in the end, discover that we have dehumanized ourselves.

The paradox is that we, who were meant to husband the earth, have broken our marriage vows. We are like those who marry selfishly for money and thereby have no real regard for the sanctity of their partners. The earth and all its fullness we have pillaged and ravished, ignoring the trust implicit in our stewardship of caring love. Blind to the ecology of our personal and our social existence we, who will not let the plants and planets live, must face the same destiny of morality and death when our material bodies return to the dust from whence they came. How ignominious is the end we face! Made by God to be only a little lower, a little less than the Elohim—the highest beings— we find ourselves refusing the ideal and choosing the impediments which lie within our being.

The paradox is that the news about men, about their private world as men and women, about their structures of society, their public institutions of law and learning, of industry and business, about their ecological existence is both good and bad. The wages of sin is death— that's the bad news. The free gift of God is eternal life through Jesus Christ, our Lord—that's the good news. We are guilty as hell—that's the bad news. Grace is greater than our sin and guilt—that's the good news. The world is mixed up, messed up—that's the bad news. The world is loved by God and reconciled to God in the cross of Christ— that's the good news. Our personal, private world is in abject bondage—that's the bad news. That world is redeemed, set free in Christ—that's the good news. Our public world is an Antichrist of dehumanizing powers and demonic forces—that's the bad news. That world has seen its false rulers deposed, its demonic powers stripped away, nailed to the cross, and Jesus Christ crowned by God as Lord and Savior—that's the good news. Because the news about ourselves, our world, and our institutions is both bad and good, each of us is faced with a personal choice of significant proportion and with eternal meaning. That choice must lead us straight into life and into personal evangelistic action.

Nowhere does the contrast between thought and deed, between reflection and action, appear to be greater than in the life of the church and its evangelistic witness. As the people of God, we study and talk together about the meaning of our Christian task. But, in the midst of all our discussion, too few of us go beyond reflection to action. Yet, we must recognize that we are to answer for our decisions and our deeds. Inaction and silence are themselves a kind of faithless absentee action which makes quite another kind of history for the world and for the church. When Jesus says, "You are my witnesses," the meaning of his statement is quite clear. No one is to be exempt; no one is to be excluded; no one is to be left out. He expects every Christian to be personally involved and to be engaged fully in the life of discipleship and in the life and work of witnessing. We are to be held accountable for our actions. For most of us, who are not preachers with convenient pulpits, our witness must find expression in person-to-person evangelism in a variety of settings.

The Protestant understanding, in our reading of the New Testament, leads us to speak of the priesthood of all believers. We believe that each Christian should expect to function as a priest to other persons, besides enjoying a direct access to God oneself. But, more than these two elements, a universal priesthood means every Christian living and acting as a witness. It suggests that, to be the pastorate of the church, the whole congregation must act together corporately as the people of God. Pastoral concern is not the minister's job alone; it is rooted and related to the concern of the entire congregation.

A universal priesthood also emphasizes that evangelism—announcing the good news—requires everyone acting in personal Christian witness. Although the gifts of the Spirit may give special equipment for specialized functions of evangelism to some persons, such as Charles Finney, John Wesley, D. L. Moody, and Billy Graham, these special gifts cannot make up or be a substitute for one's own witness as a Christian if it is withheld.

In the sixth chapter of the book of Acts in the New Testament, we read about an incident in the early church at Jerusalem, which illumines the theme of this chapter. A controversy had arisen between the Hebrew and the Hellenistic believers. The Hellenists felt that their widows were being neglected in the ministry of relief. To settle this dispute, the apostles came up with a plan which they asked the whole church to endorse. "It is not right," the apostles said, "that we should give up preaching the word of God to serve tables" (Acts 6:2). In the light of that conviction, they suggested that seven men of good reputation and filled with the Holy Spirit should be selected and placed in charge of this special service. The plan was approved by the church, and seven deacons were elected to wait on the tables and to relieve the apostles so that they could devote themselves completely to what they described as the ministry of prayer and of the word.

However, it appears that God acted quickly to upset the dangerous precedent of having two classes of people in the church: one a special elite who would be responsible for announcing the good news and for praying and witnessing, and, then, a second class to render a more restricted service ministry. In the seventh chapter of Acts, we read the amazing account of what the Spirit of God led Stephen to do as he became the first martyr of the church. Then, in Acts, chapter 8, we read another remarkable account of how God led Philip to Samaria and then beyond Samaria in effective person-to-person witness. It is as though God wishes to upset any definition, which assumes that some Christians can be relegated to ecclesiastical housekeeping chores or to relatively trivial and unimportant roles in the church.

We must conclude that every Christian is called to share in the task of witness and that every Christian has a witness to give. All of us are to be "good news people" who know what the good news is. We know it is meant for the whole world, for everyone, everywhere, and we know that the good news is meant for the whole person. Beyond that, we could go on to say that "good news people" are themselves the firstfruits of the gospel. They are meant to be more than a pipeline through which a message flows. The message is designed to bring about significant changes in the life and character of the messenger himself. We may speak of these profound personal transformations as embracing "an Evangelistic Life Style." What does it mean for us as good news people to have an evangelistic life style?

This life style means to come of age and to accept our responsibility and accountability for learning to share the good news with everyone, everywhere that we live. If we ask ourselves the question "Why should I tell the good news?" what we really may be asking is, "How can I tell the good news?" Most Christians appear to be living with an uneasy conscience because they know that they are under a mandate to be witnesses for Jesus Christ. Like the four lepers in the Old Testament on the day when severe famine ended, we find ourselves confessing, "We are not doing right. This day is a day of good news; if we are silent . . . punishment will overtake us . . ." (2 Kings 7:9).

One of the main reasons that we are silent is because we may feel unqualified for our task of Christian witnessing. No one has really taken time to help us get ready for that momentous assignment. Some of us may feel disqualified because we are not quite clear as to what we, ourselves, were being asked to become or to do when we were first invited to believe and to acknowledge Christ as Lord and Savior. The life style of many Christians seems to be very much like that of their unconverted neighbors. We may find ourselves asking, "How can I witness to my neighbors unless there is a measurable difference between us in terms of our value systems and in our relationship to the world and our use of life?"

In the chapters to follow, I want to speak to these feelings of uncertainty which are all too common among us as God's people. I want to help you to fill out the picture of what it means to live with a distinctive "Evangelistic Life Style" of your own. I want also to help amplify your understanding of what a decision for Jesus Christ means, in terms of both his saving grace and his lordship. The purpose of our study is to lead each person to make a covenant decision which can lead him to accept the evangelistic task and trust which are vested in the life and faith of every Christian believer.

The movement which is now stirring in our midst is long overdue. For too long a time we, like the fearful Christians in Jerusalem, have been settled down behind locked doors. Now there is a fresh word coming to us another time as it did centuries ago to faithless Jonah, to a denying Peter, and to a feckless John Mark. Instead of Ichabod (The glory of God is departed [1 Samuel 4:21]) being etched over the doors of our temples, our churches, and our lives, we see another word inscribed. It is a word of hope and promise, as God writes: "Behold, I make all things new." In an era of bad news, Christians have good news to tell. The world, long since misbegotten by man's marriage to the goddess of selfish pride, is to be mended by Christ's liberating lordship and creative power. The gospel, too long forgotten, once again will be on the lips of God's people, because it comes to them in their hearts and minds, as a word of faith and hope and love: good news for everyone, everywhere.

This world, which God had made, was very good; in all its parts complete, its order stood, a witness to its Maker's handiwork before the earth with evil went berserk. Within the realm of time, man's life sublime reflected perfect goodness in each clime; a symbol of God's providence in space, which keeps the planets orbiting in place. But, to this world which knew no lack of good—where beauty filled its gardens and its woods—a tempter came and stood, as one without, and whispered in man's ear discordant doubt: "Has God withheld some freedom from your view? Why does he choose to limit your milieu? Is it because you'll be as free as he? Why should such dread restrict your liberty?" Encouraged thus, as rebels, by these words, man's action brought creation the absurd. As chaos once again emerged from fall, and death began to reign in shadowed pall, the world of nature lapsed into decay, as men grew distant to their Maker's way. So did the bloom of beauty turn to blight, and discord filled the minds of men with fright. This planet earth, which God had made once good, is seen as prisoner, waiting death row's hood; damned, with no pardon for its conviction; salvation means man's cosmic eviction! Let us now protest this predicted end which sees for misbegotten worlds no mend. Did God not promise us a woman's seed, who would redeem this world with cosmic deed? So, let the fullness of our faith declare that God incarnate in the flesh did bear the burden of the world's regret and care, renewing worlds askew, his love forbears. So then, at last, earth's chaos time will pass, as cosmos faith gives shape to purpose vast: Christ will be truth which makes men free as he; Christ will be life, his way earth's destiny!

2 | Good News— Promise and Event

The Bible is a book filled with a message of good news for everyone everywhere because it speaks of the promise of God, given to the world as his response to the bad news of our human predicament.

When Jesus came into the world in the days of his flesh, the New Testament interpreted the event as the grace of God appearing (Titus 2:11–3:7). Jesus did not come to *make* God gracious; he came because God *is* gracious. Hence, Jesus is spoken of as the lamb who was slain before the foundation of the world (see 1 Peter 1:19-20), signifying that God's purposes of grace antedate human history itself. The best that we know about God we see in the event of Christ in the New Testament, which fulfills the earlier promises of the Old Testament. But, in his essential character, God has never been less than what we see him revealed to be in Christ. The event of Christ, in terms of purpose and mission, was to reconcile the world to God; because it was the world, not God, which was filled with the bad news of alienation and brokenness. Great is the mystery of godliness—God was manifest in the flesh. The gospel of Jesus Christ is the good news of God's promise, now fulfilled in the event of Christ as he was born of a woman, made under the law, acting to redeem those under the law.

To understand the meaning of our Christian hope in our person-to-person witness, let us review six fundamental events related to the expression of the good news: (1) Christmas, (2) Good Friday, (3) Easter, (4) Ascension, (5) Pentecost, and (6) Parousia.

1. *Christmas*—centered in the life of Jesus born at Bethlehem—is

the good news of incarnation, when the Word became flesh, dwelling in the midst of human history. The Christmas event is the good news that the course of history is interruptible. God is not a prisoner outside of his universe, but he is shown as its maker, sustainer, and redeemer. All things are made through him and by him and for him. The humanity of Jesus Christ reveals to us that the world of nature and of history is more than a temporary stage on which Jesus makes a brief appearance. The whole creation shares in the redemptive story and awaits its own release from bondage to decay. History is not a meaningless merry-go-round on which men ride inexorably to oblivion because the good news of Christmas assures us that this is a visited planet.

Christ has come with love to identify himself with us and our situation and to reverse the effects of the first sin and disobedience and the fruits of all our woe. The doom of nature is lifted; the demonic forces of evil in the world are put on notice that they are destined to be deposed. Christ comes to announce God's Year of Jubilee! His name is Jesus because he saves his people from their sins. God's salvation means wholeness, restoring to us our integrity in the private, social, and public dimensions and sectors of our divided being. Christmas— Bethlehem—incarnation—tell us that history has been interrupted by God's own intervention in Jesus Christ! As a result, life gains a new direction, a new meaning, and a new promise which we have in hope like an anchor behind the veil. That's the good news we can share in our person-to-person witness.

2. *Good Friday*—the death of Jesus on the cross of Calvary—is the good news that alienation is reconcilable. The predicament of humanity, since the exile from Eden, has been the estrangement from God, together with our alienation from ourselves, our neighbors, and our world. In spiritual isolation, persons became nameless and rootless, without God and without hope in the world. As a consequence, personal anonymity led to social alienation, whereby we fractured the unity intended by God in the human family. Torn by a civil war within, with the loss of our personal integrity and identity, we abandoned the created spheres of interdependence and mutuality. Forces of hate and hostility produced fear and suspicion among us. Proving false to the stewardship trust given to us in creation, we abandoned our care of the earth, so that greed and selfishness characterized our plans and our actions.

But, the cross of Christ is the good news that God was in Christ, reconciling the world unto himself. The cross is the good news that alienation is reconcilable. God has acted to upset the entrenched powers of evil. He has crushed the devil and the powers of sin and death (Hebrews 2:14-15). He has spoiled principalities and powers, nailing them to the cross and to an open shame (Colossians 1:16-20). He has acted in Christ to break down the middle wall of partition and to fashion one new humanity (Ephesians 2). He has abolished death and has shed light on life. Good Friday celebrates the death of Jesus on the cross of Calvary because the cosmic deed contains the good news that alienation is reconcilable; the world is redeemable. That's part of the good news which we share in our person-to-person witness.

3. *Easter*—the resurrection of Jesus Christ from Joseph's garden tomb—is the good news that the future is believable. The good news of resurrection is that Jesus Christ is alive as a living Savior, the author of an eternal salvation, declared to be the Son of God with power, so that he is able to save unto the uttermost and to the end of time all those who come to God by him. The basis of this Christian hope, which makes the future for us both open and believable, is the fact that Jesus Christ is alive forevermore. He offers to us his mercy and his grace and his abiding presence. In the reality of his forgiveness, we know ourselves adopted into the family of God, no longer strangers, aliens, or orphans. In the resurrection of Jesus, God pledges to us that death itself has been conquered so that our beloved dead are not lost to us.

We receive the confident assurance that the future is open to us wherein God will fulfill the promise of our hope, so that our past failures need not be final; and the last word is not death and despair, but life and meaning. The good news of resurrection is the reality of a hope that we have, assuring us that a new future begins here and now and will lead to the fulfillment of our unfulfilled losses. Christ overshadows our sense of personal incompleteness; we know we are destined to be complete in him. The future belongs to us now by faith, and we are drawn into it by the power and the promise of his confidence. Withheld completions of life shall one day be explained, together with the meaning of our pain. Because Christ lives forever, all the tenses of human life—past, present, and future—are summed up in him. He is the same yesterday, today, and forever.

The Christian hope speaks, therefore, not only of eternal life for the believer, but also of *new* heavens and a *new* earth! The Christian hope includes the completion of *all* that God began in creation.

The resurrection of Jesus not only means the death of death, but it means also the death of every despotism which rules the world and the affairs of men and nations with inequity and injustice. Easter is the good news that Jesus had the power to lay down his life, but he had the power also to take it up again. Because Christ is risen, faith is both vindicated and victorious. Thanks be to God who leads us in the train of Christ's triumph! We can share that faith and hope in our person-to-person witness as the good news of Easter; because God is faithful—death and evil could not triumph over the truth of Jesus without destroying the faithfulness of God. Hence, the New Testament declares, it was not possible for Jesus to be held by death!

4. *Ascension*—the glorification of Jesus Christ from the brow of Olivet—is the good news of Christ's lordship in the church, over the world, and in us as persons. Ascension does not mean that he has forsaken history, but, that after suffering and death and resurrection, he is exalted at the right hand of the Father where we see him crowned with glory and honor, both Lord and Christ. In the words of the early apostolic testimony, ". . . there is another king, Jesus" (Acts 17:7). This is bad news to the despotisms and the false rulers of the age, but it is good news to the world and to us. As Lord of history, even as he is the light of the world and the life of the church, Jesus Christ has the right to reign. He has a right to rule and overrule. He has a right to requisition what we are and what we have, to claim it for his service (1 Samuel 8:9-17). The exaltation of Jesus Christ signifies to us the good news that God is working in everything, everywhere, to achieve his eternal purpose that his will may be done on the earth and in the affairs of people and of nations, even as it is done in heaven.

Because the destinies of history are linked to the purposes of heaven, everyone and everything is accountable to him. The secrets we hold shall be judged by Jesus Christ and his gospel. What we do privately, what we do socially, and what we do in the public realm, in institutions, and in society—everything stands under the judgment of Christ who reveals himself as God's true plumb line of justice. He will maintain the order and the justice of the world, and he shall measure out justice and judgment wherever it is due.

Ascension is the good news that Jesus Christ, having been born of a woman and having lived under the law, is now himself the law of truth and the King of the ages. Just as the image on the Roman coin reminded people that they belonged to Caesar and lived under his dominion, so the image of God in us, marred by sin but recast in the image of Jesus Christ, symbolizes that we and our world belong to him. Whether we live or die, we are his. The good news of ascension, which we share in our person-to-person witness, is that the world has another King and his name is Jesus. We, in the life of the church, together with the nations of the world, are accountable to him and his dominion. We do not make him Lord; he is Lord. It is *our* decision to acknowledge, to accept, and to confess as did the apostle Thomas, "My Lord and my God."

5. *Pentecost*—sent as the earnest and the firstfruits of the new age inaugurated by Christ—is the good news of the presence of God's own Spirit. Pentecost is the good news that Christian community is actualized in Christ and is meant to be unbreakable. Just as the Tower of Babel symbolized the fateful divisions which divided people in selfishness and incoherence from their common life, Pentecost is the sign of the single new humanity, created in Christ, who is its life-giving spirit. Age-old animosities and walls of division are broken down. From lives of false sufficiency and superiority, the human family is destined to regain its sense of mutual interdependence intended by God, as in the first creation. The new community reflects the common creation of which the Bible speaks. We have all one Father (Malachi 2:10). We are all made of one blood (Acts 17:26). Because one is our Father, we are brethren (Matthew 23:9; John 8:41). The paradoxical uniqueness and unity of the human family is the gift of God's creative hand (Genesis 1:26-28).

The community created in Christ also reflects the continuity of God's covenant forming the people of God. The people that were no people are now God's people (Hosea 1:8-11; 1 Peter 2:9-10). In Christ, God has acted to renew the covenant, as foretold by Jeremiah (Jeremiah 31:33-34). The new community in Christ is brought into being by his reconciling action on the cross (Ephesians 2:14-16; Galatians 3:28). The new covenant community created by Christ involves continuing decisions in response to continuing demand. We announce God's Year of Jubilee (Luke 4:18-19); we respond to God's persistent question: "Where is your brother?" We love God whom we have not seen by loving our brother and serving our neighbor (1 John 4:19-21; 1 John 3:17-18; Matthew 25). We share in the community formed by the companionship of God's own Spirit, which provides interior resources which do not fail (Romans 8:26; 1 John 5:4-5). In God's strength, we gain courage to stand against the dehumanizing, demonic powers of the universe and to honor the stewardship entrusted to us to build and to renew the earth. Living together as joint heirs in Christ, we refuse to parcel out our inheritance as though it is to be enjoyed alone (Romans 8:16-17; 1 Peter 3:7).

The strong ties of our Christian community set us free to participate in the life of the world, cooperating with its instruments and agencies to help humanize its life. Such cooperation is made imperative, because we have learned in Christ that no one is excluded from God's redemptive purpose, even though all have not yet accepted it (1 John 2:2; Romans 10:12; Acts 10:34). Pentecost is the good news that, just as there is one biology common to us as persons, so there is one biosphere common to our world. We drink our water from a common well; we are fed by the produce of the one fertile earth. We are bound up together in the bundle of life, interdependent in relationship to nature and to our common destiny. In our person-to-person witness, we share the good news of Pentecost, the power of the Spirit's presence to make Christian community in the human family actual and unbreakable.

6. *Parousia*—in the eschatology of Patmos and the Second Advent—is the good news that God's eternal purposes are unshakable and undefeatable. The word *parousia* meant literally "to be with," so that Parousia has come to mean the Lord's appearing. Eschatology is the doctrine of last things. So Jesus is the sum of all things and offers us our surest clue into the future.

The book of Revelation, in the midst of its Oriental imagery and apocalyptic language, pictures Jesus in heaven breaking the seals which no one else could open. He is shown as the Final Person of the universe, because the eternal purpose of God has been established to sum up *all* things in Christ. He is worthy because he has suffered, but he has triumphed in his pain. He is worthy because he has been granted the keys unlocking the mysteries of human existence and the issues of life and death. We have already seen that, in the cross and resurrection of Jesus, God has acted so that Jesus emerged in victory. The Second Advent of Jesus will be to consummate the new age, which he brought with him at his first coming. The Second Advent of Jesus will complete the whole process of human history and cosmic purpose, which we see in the life and work of Christ already.

Meanwhile, we are faced with the question addressed to the disciples in the book of Acts, "Men of Galilee, why do you stand looking into heaven? This Jesus . . . will come in the same way as you saw him go into heaven" (Acts 1:11). They were losing the limited and local presence of the Christ so that they might gain the living and universal presence and power of Christ's Spirit. But then they were enjoined to move from idol adoration to faithful Christian action and witness. The good news involved in the Parousia, envisioned by John on the Isle of Patmos, is that the kingdom of Christ is founded on the undefeatable purpose of God. It moves from the particular to the universal; from the local to the ecumenical, involving the whole inhabited earth; from the nominal and marginal to the total achievement of all that was in God's heart and mind at the foundation of the world. God's purposes in redemption will complete the intent of his first creation and will include not only our own personal salvation but also new heavens and a new earth. Babylon will yield to the presence and to the reality of the new Jerusalem. The gates of hell itself cannot stand against the power of Christ's kingdom.

Hence, the book· of Revelation testifies that the kingdoms of this world are to become the kingdoms of our Lord and his Christ. To paraphrase, "The power to rule over the world belongs now to our Lord and His Messiah, and He will rule forever and ever" (see Revelation 11:15, author's paraphrase). Even so, the apostle Paul certifies that as we eagerly wait for our Savior, the Lord Jesus Christ, to come from heaven, his power to change our weak mortal bodies and make them like his own glorious body will be achieved by his use of that power by which he is able to bring all things under his rule (Philippians 3:20-21). Parousia is the good news we can share in our person-to-person witness that the eternal purposes of God remain unshakable and undefeatable. Beginning with us as persons and extending to the farthest reaches of the cosmic spheres, "Behold," God says, "I am making all things new."

In conclusion, then, let us summarize the good news which we have to share about Jesus Christ with the whole world and with the whole person. At Bethlehem in Christmas, he interrupts history and acts to reconstitute the nature and destiny of people and nations. At Calvary, in his cross, he reconciles all things to himself, effecting redemption on a cosmic scale. At Easter, from Joseph's garden tomb, he conquers death, opening up and confirming the future to us with hope. At his ascension from Olivet's brow, he confiscates the spoils of sin and death and claims his rightful place as Lord and Christ. At Pentecost, he creates the new community as the continuing body of Christ to serve as the instrument of the new creation. At Patmos, in the promised Parousia and Advent, he is revealed, completing and consummating the eternal purposes of God, so that God may be in all and with all. This is the beginning of the good news in our own perception, experience, and understanding of all that Jesus began both to do and to teach. There is much more to follow as we share the good news with everyone, everywhere, and with the whole person.

3 | Good News for Everyone, Everywhere

The American Bible Society's title of the New Testament in Today's English Version is *Good News for Modern Man.* The cover carries more than the title of the New Testament itself. One sees there also the mastheads of several newspapers from different parts of the world: *The Atlanta Journal, The New York Times, The Times of India, The Japan Times,* the *East African Standard, The Sydney Morning Herald,* and others. If we ask what this cover is meant to symbolize, one could say that the Bible, in today's language, is as up-to-date as today's newspaper! Another analogy would be that the message of the Bible is international and cosmopolitan. Its message is not limited to any one land or people, nor could it be confined to a single culture. The title, *Good News for Modern Man,* also suggests that, if the newspapers of the world are filled with the bad news about hate and rape, murder and mayhem, political intrigue, wars and rumors of war, the Bible also contains an honest description of people at their best and at their worst. Beyond all this, a further analogy could say that the Bible, like these daily newspapers, records and reports the news about people, their ideas, their actions, and their deeds. The Bible is an historical record of real people in real life. But what makes the Bible unique is that it contains the best of news about the redeeming presence of God's love in the midst of human life. That means Good News for everyone, everywhere!

The New Testament leaves no room for doubt that God means the good news to be widely published to everyone, everywhere. The words of Jesus in Matthew 28:16-20, found in similar forms in each of the Gospels, reveal that the world map of Jesus extends to the far corners of the earth—east, west, north, and south! Most of us in the church have no trouble accepting the imperative for missionary outreach into other lands and culture. Our personal difficulty resides in being able to function effectively as a witness to our neighbor across the street, at school, on the job, or in our family. Yet, we find Jesus persistently reminding us, "You are my witnesses"—beginning where you are (Acts 1:8). We cannot elude or shake off the sense of his claim, knowing that he expects us to be personally involved in heralding the good news to everyone, everywhere. Like the Gospel of John, our faith is meant to be instrumental in leading others to find life in his name. (See John 20:31.) In the light of this task, how can we get a better grasp on the good news for ourselves so that we can become more effective in our evangelistic, person-to-person witness?

To reply to our common concern, it needs to be said that the sense of urgency we should feel in behalf of the gospel and our evangelistic task is not because the gospel is something we have to manufacture and ship FOB from where we live. Christians do not make up the good news; they receive the good news in Christ and find it validated in their lives and in their community of faith and in their witness. For this reason, we do not need to be anxious about the order of the words which we are led to use in witnessing for Christ. The gospel must be put in words to be explained; that is true enough, but the gospel events are vital realities more than they are verbal rigidities. The good news is a message centered, not in the immovable type of a printed page, but in the moving testimony of a personal proclamation. The apostle Paul helps us to understand that fact when he draws a contrast between his own situation and the living word of God. He, himself, is shut up in prison, but he writes: "The word of God is not fettered" (2 Timothy 2:9). You can put the *prophets* of God in prison, but you cannot imprison the *promises* of God. You can bind and fetter God's messengers, but you can't put chains on God's living Spirit.

We have good news to tell because, although we know it best in its verbal form, it becomes a vital life and message which cannot be managed or manipulated by us. The real word of God is not locked up inside a book, not even in our favorite translations of the Bible. Nor can the living Word be locked up inside our ecclesiastical forms and liturgies and organizations; the living Word of God is stronger than any two-edged sword. Penetrating are its insights and judgments, so that the Word of God has an effective life of its own, quite apart from your initiative or mine as Christian believers and witnesses.

The living Word is none other than the voice of the living God, who speaks to us as he calls us by our own names and summons us to faith, to decision, which leads to a new life in Christ. That new style of life, with its wholeness and integrity, its sense of interdependent community and its acceptance of a stewardship trust for the world, is what I shall be describing throughout this book as an "Evangelistic Life Style." But, in that new life style, we shall find that, just as Jesus Christ, himself, is the good news, so today for us the Spirit of God is the Evangelist. Our task is to bear a confirming sign and witness which asks our friends and neighbors everywhere, "Have you heard the good news?"

In our person-to-person witness task, we may find it possible to help those who have regarded the good news as an irrelevant distraction. These people may ask in a variety of ways, "How can a person like Jesus Christ, born in the first century, be good news for me living in the last part of the twentieth century?" Behind that recurring question are the feelings of these people who have experienced several kinds of future shock in their lives. Some textbooks which they have used in earlier school days have long since become obsolete. And there are many people, like engineers and scientists, whose knowledge will become obsolescent in the course of their professional careers unless they find it possible to keep pace with the knowledge explosion. So they feel that their question, as they seek to cope with the meaning of change, is quite appropriate. How *can* a first-century Christ satisfy the questions and the feelings and the needs of twentieth-century people?

How can we reply? We can say that Christ remains relevant to our own age because he, himself, is ageless. Although he was born in Palestine and lived most of his life within the narrow boundaries of that land, we do not see Jesus limited and local, as much as we discover him to be cosmopolitan and universal. Jesus stands at the center of the calendar as an inexhaustible person, born in the fullness of time at the end of an old age so that he might inaugurate a new age of divine grace.

An illustration of this may be found in one of his own words when he says of himself, "I am the Alpha and the Omega" (Revelation 1:8). Alpha and Omega are the first and the last letters in the Greek alphabet and would correspond to the letters "A" and "Z" in our English alphabet. To put these words of Jesus in contemporary language would be to hear him say, "I am the 'A' and the 'Z.'" In effect, he is claiming to be the whole alphabet. One is led to remember that, despite the millions of volumes which have been published and which rest upon all of our library shelves, these books have all been written by people using only twenty-six letters of the English alphabet to form their nouns and verbs and adjectives and adverbs. The alphabet, itself, remains inexhaustible. Despite the passing of time, the alphabet is dateless and does not lose its meaning in our own decade.

In much the same way, Jesus Christ, born in the first century, is revealed as the Author of an eternal salvation, central to every century, accessible to every age, generic to every human generation. We can't outdistance him; he goes before us to lead the way. We can't outgrow him. Instead, we strive to advance to the fullness of his stature. We are still living out of his inexhaustible fullness. Once we begin to recognize the universal meaning of his life, we begin to sense why he is able to satisfy the hungers and the feelings of our own age as he has done in all earlier periods of human history.

One of the common feelings we encounter in people today is that the world is like a vast orphanage, or some big, complex machine. These feelings, in part, may be the product of our scientific method which explains so much about life on the basis of cause and effect. Moreover, all of our discoveries which have revealed the immensity of space and the size of the universe have made many people recognize that they no longer seem to be standing at the center of it all. If the world is like some great machine running all by itself, that explanation seems to push God off from the center of things out into the margins of life. And, if people themselves are dwarfed and orphaned in a world where Mother Nature is dumb, even though she may be beautiful, that explains much of the reason why they experience alienation and rootlessness. Abandoned, unwanted, and feeling unloved, people see themselves as orphans.

At this very point Christ touches us with his saving love and help. Christ meets us at the very point of our alienation and assures us that he has reconciled us to God. At long last, we can be reconciled to our distant selves. Though we are abandoned and unloved, Christ meets us at the point of our homesickness and assures us that God's love has adopted us and has brought us inside the family as a full member. Though we are rootless and rejected, Christ meets us at the point of our rejection to tell us that we have been received and are fully accepted in the Father's family. So Christ comes to speak to us who feel ourselves as orphans, and he shows us God as a caring heavenly Father and his church as our spiritual mother. Christ meets us at the point of our needs and our unsatisfied longings. If we feel unfulfilled, he provides us a new beginning which completes our haunting sense of incompleteness. As the Author of an eternal salvation, he is able to meet and satisfy the homesick feelings of the people in our age, to whom we are destined to carry our Christian witness.

We can describe another set of feelings which are very much a part of the contemporary mood in our age. Many other people feel as if they are trapped by their circumstances in a situation where there is no way out. In fact, this is so much a part of the way that today's people feel that a contemporary playwright has a drama entitled *No Exit.* These feelings of being trapped or being hemmed in, where power to act no longer seems to make much sense, help to explain why our age is pockmarked with cynicism, hopelessness, despair, aggression, and violence. Camus, the French dramatist, in his story entitled *The Fall,* depicts the abject despair of a man who discovers his incapacity to respond to the call of another human being, a lonely call for help from a young woman drowning in a canal. Camus tells us that the crisis of all men and women in our contemporary age is due to the search for a human response by those who themsclvcs seem unable to respond.

To this widespread feeling of being trapped by the determinism of life or fate, Christ comes with a word of deliverance and of hope. At the beginning of his public ministry, he announced he was the great liberator, ushering in God's Year of Jubilee, which gave to slaves their freedom, emancipated the oppressed from their oppressors, and redistributed the spoils of injustice. So he comes to us today where we are trapped by our past sins and old failures, and he provides for us a way out, an exit, a door of faith. Forgiveness is the gift of God which sets us free from our sin and our experience of guilt.

"I thank God," the apostle Paul says, "there is a way out through Jesus Christ." (See Romans 7:25.) Christ is the door which leads to life, life that is abundantly full. Because he is our eternal contemporary, he replenishes our exhausted supply of strength. Instead of our finding Christ to be a sedative, he comes to us as God's salvation and as a solution to problems; he awakens our vital being and exhilarates all of life. Satisfying the hunger of the human heart in its private aspects, fulfilling our need of the social self for community, and leading us into a life of love and service in our institutional and corporate memberships, Christ abides, adequate and up-to-date. That's part of our testimony which we are to give in our person-to-person witness.

If we are to be effective witnesses, we must cut through the thickets which have grown up around grace and gospel to hedge others out and to keep ourselves safe. The good news is not a religious code to be imposed upon us; instead the good news is Jesus Christ becoming real to us as Lord and Savior and inviting us to follow him. At the outset, Christians were described as followers of the Way. The gospel is good news because it comes to assure us of God's unconditional acceptance. We are, the Bible tells us, "accepted in the beloved" (Ephesians 1:6, KJV). God knows all about us, including our faults and our failures, our temptations and our moral weaknesses. He knows about our secret thoughts and the hidden flaws of our character. He sees our sins by day and by night. He knows when we are sick of ourselves. Yet he assures us that, although we are unacceptable to ourselves or to others, his love accepts us unconditionally in the life and the love of Christ. The Bible reminds us that "God sent the Son into the world, not to condemn the world, but that the world might be saved through him" (John 3:17). With unwearied and undiscourageable power, God's love reaches into our lives to prove to us that, whatever our past and however hopeless our present situation may seem, however unlovable we are, however unacceptable, his love is able to break down all the barriers which shut him out; and his love accepts us fully in Christ.

We recognize that because the good news is grace it seems incredible. No wonder some have not really heard it or understood it. But when we are led to accept the truth of our acceptance in Jesus Christ, whose coming into the world has made God's love most clearly visible, *everything* about our situation begins to reflect the changed conditions and the relationships we now enjoy. Before, we hated ourselves and found it difficult to accept ourselves with honesty. We found it necessary to cloak and hide our faults and to justify our sins. We found it necessary in some ways to punish ourselves. Unconsciously we told ourselves, somebody has to pay for sin, and since we did not know that our sins were already paid for in full, we tried persistently to find ways to atone for our failures and our mistakes. The love of God is paradoxical because while he loves the whole world, yet his love is made local in our lives. He singles us out of the faceless crowd and knows us by our own names, just as Jesus saw Zacchaeus amid the throngs of people and individualized him by his name: "Zacchaeus, I must spend today at your house."

God's love is able to break in upon our routine days and to pervade the natural order of life, so that we can be complete in Christ, in body, soul, and spirit and in our private, social, and public dimensions of personal identity and integrity.

4 | Good News for the Whole Person

In *Main Street and the Mind of God,* I have sought to explain how we as the people of God on mission cannot afford to be absent from history because it is there that we find the living God at work in behalf of his eternal purposes, so that his will may be done on earth as it is in heaven. I have sought to interpret our evangelistic task with a wide-angle lens, involving both a private and a public import and impact, reflecting incarnational as well as inward dimensions, social and personal meanings of equal validity, pastoral and prophetic concerns of equal scope, leading us to satisfy both priestly and political aspects of the Christian witness, ministry, and service.[1] I believe that many of the fruitless debates among Christians which preempted our personal availability for mission have been ended, and that we are ready now to accept the evangelistic ministry entrusted to us by Christ in its fullest and in its deepest sense.

I am reminded, however, of a valid point made by A.N. Whitehead in one of his essays on the rhythm of education. He tells us that in many places a familiar law of learning, which sees us moving from the simple to the complex, is upset and abrogated in practical experience. For example, we ask our children at a very young age to perform two of the most difficult learning tasks long before one could hope that they would be ready in terms of age. First, we ask them to acquire a spoken language which is the correlation of meaning with sounds. Next, we require them to learn a written language, which demands

---

[1]William F. Keucher, *Main Street and the Mind of God* (Valley Forge: Judson Press, 1974), especially chap. 6.

the more difficult task of correlating meaning with shapes and symbols! On the basis of complexity and difficulty, one should expect that these two learning tasks would be postponed to a much later period in the child's life in his process of education and learning. Why, then, do these tasks come so early?

As Whitehead concludes, they come first because they are elemental to the whole learning process which is to follow. They come first because they are first.

So it is in our evangelistic mission that there are some tasks which cannot be postponed until a later time when we might be older, wiser, and more ready. One such task is that of person-to-person evangelistic witness, whereby the story is passed along from life to life, face to face, and from mind to mind and from heart to heart. Our task of presenting Jesus Christ and the adequacy of his claims, of announcing the good news winsomely and effectively, so that others may be led by God's Spirit to make a personal and public profession of their own faith in Christ as Lord and Savior—that task stands first and foremost in our midst in the church. Person-to-person witnessing is not like a second fork on a nicely laid table. It is an essential and basic utensil with which we must begin. Personal evangelism comes first because it is first. It is not like luxury equipment added to the vehicle; it is the vehicle. It claims us at the outset because it stands at every threshold like a door whose bell keeps ringing, waiting for our answer. It has a priority because we are dealing with the beginning of Christian experience and life. The urgency of witnessing resides in the nature of the good news itself, which insists on prolonging itself, as P. T. Forsyth reminded us, like the tides which come in again and again; and the urgency resides within the nature of our own faithful response. Witnessing is an imperative task because it has been laid upon us as God's people by an imperial command. The task is never fully discharged in time or space because it comes fresh to every new generation while, at the same time, it has an eternal and universal content which transcends the borders of existing nations and structures.

To speak about assigning a priority to person-to-person evangelism does not mean that we are denying the value and the validity of other realities and items in our Christian mission and their scale. But, in assigning a priority to person-to-person evangelistic witness, we are challenging the mechanical views which are widely held as to how personal decisions are made for Christ and how our witness itself is most effectively shared. For example, I am not subscribing to the ladder theory of learning, which sees a person starting at the bottom and climbing to the top, rung by rung. In this distorted view of how we learn, grow, and change in our choices and commitments, it was traditionally assumed that first comes Christian conversion in evangelism. That represented the first rung. Next comes Christian growth, the second rung; next comes Christian service, a third rung; next comes social action, a fourth rung, as converted people work transforming society; next comes institutional change, as Christians change the organizational aims and structures in which they work. That was the fifth rung. The last rung of all was regarded as global change, which takes place through the Christian presence and action and influence in international agencies and governments.

The fact that this vision has persisted so long tells us that there is enough truth mixed with error so that we have passed along the concepts from one year to the next. What's wrong with this perception of Christian witness, rung by rung?

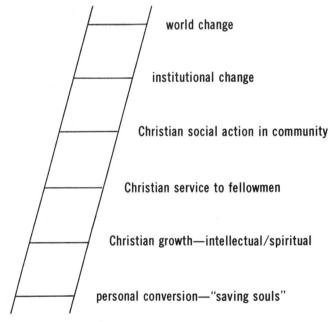

world change

institutional change

Christian social action in community

Christian service to fellowmen

Christian growth—intellectual/spiritual

personal conversion—"saving souls"

The basic fallacy involved in this picture is that it misrepresents the aspects of what it means to be a person, and it artificially separates some realities of our personal being and human existence which belong together in our essential identity and integrity. A second fallacy is that this paradigm misunderstands the meaning of God's salvation. "Soul" is misunderstood to represent the spirituality of a person. This paradigm misrepresents and seriously distorts the biblical understanding of salvation by limiting it to the unseen part of our personal existence.

In the biblical account of creation in Genesis, it is clear that to be a person is, first, to have bodily existence; second, it is to be "inbreathed" by the Spirit of God; third, the product of this creative fusion of matter plus spirit is described as "soul." God fashioned man's body out of the dust of the earth, breathed into this new creation the breath, the Spirit of his own life, and "man became a living soul" (Genesis 2:7, KJV). The biblical account reminds us that "man" was not used to describe his sexual denotation, but that it is the word which describes "humanity." The Bible explains "male and female he created them" as God makes humanity in his own image and likeness (Genesis 1:26-27). Why does the Bible speak of humanity in plurality, rather than man in the singular? Because, we are told, "The Lord God said, 'It is not good that the man should be alone'" (Genesis 2:18).

According to the biblical understanding, then, to speak about the saving of the soul does not mean to save the invisible or the inside part of a man's being, or the private part of his person. It is to save the *whole* man. The whole personhood of man is involved in God's saving action. The whole being and the context of our total existence—private, social, and public—must be included in our personal decision to accept Jesus Christ as our Lord and Savior. To understand the wholeness of God's salvation as reflected in the Bible is to understand why the biblical witness gives so much importance to the body. Instead of settling for the idea of the immortality of the soul, which could easily dispense with the human body, we are given the biblical hope in Christ of resurrection. We are promised "new bodies . . . that will never be sick again and will never die" (Romans 8:23, *The Living Bible*).

The ladder picture of personal existence tends to divide the unity of man's personality into separate and marginal parts, each on a different rung. This idea perhaps emerges from the influence of Greek humanism and idealism, which regarded the human body as a principal of individuation. What distinguished souls was the fact that each had a body. The distinctive body was theirs by fate, with its innate drives and its fated limitations.

To the contrary, the biblical view of humanity—"male and female"—regards the body as our means of social solidarity. Bodily existence is a vital part of personal existence in relation to the family, to the community, to our social and our public selves, and to the world of nature itself. The biblical account of creation roots man in nature, in community, in temporal history as a maker of culture, and in a face-to-face relationship to God, enjoying an unbroken filial fellowship to his fatherly goodness. This network is so close to us as persons that our personality itself cannot develop fully or healthily if we are isolated or insulated from any of these contextual linkages and meanings.

When the perfect human life of Jesus is described in the New Testament by Luke, it is said that he grew in stature, in wisdom, and in favor with God and man (see Luke 2:52). His physical growth related him to real nature. His spiritual growth reflected his unbroken communion with the Father, while his social growth evidenced his solidarity with the people from whose stock he came in human form, the covenant community of faith by which they were constituted in response to God's call. His growth in wisdom relates him to culture and history in the public realm of human existence. The miracle of Jesus, in part, is his being the fullness of God in the body of his incarnation. We see him as both local and universal. His humanity is so real that you can see him, hear him, and touch him, while he stands in every culture and century and country as ageless and universal— God's representative man. To speak of him, therefore, as God's representative man is to say that Jesus embodies the perfect revelation of the new creation, the new humanity, including the best of both genders.

This picture of Jesus' human development should not be lost to us because it is a vivid biblical illustration of what it means for us to be saved. The Bible tells us that the purpose of God's redemption is to fulfill the original concerns of his creation (see Acts 15:14-18, Moffatt). The Bible presents a hope that our ultimate goal and destiny is that we ourselves will one day be like Jesus Christ because we shall see him as he is (1 John 3:2). When, therefore, the apostle Paul is led to describe the purpose of Christian ministry for which the people of God are fully equipped by the presence and gifts of God's own Spirit, what is he led to say? God's gifts, he points out, are to equip all of God's people for the work of Christian service to build up the body of Christ. That takes place as "we all attain to the unity of the faith and of the knowledge of the Son of God, to mature manhood, to the measure of the stature of the fulness of Christ" (Ephesians 4:11-13).

Let us be clear that a decision for Jesus Christ which brings us into the salvation of God means wholeness and completeness. We are not to be marginally saved or partially saved. Our private selves cannot be saved at the expense of our social or our public selves. Our public selves cannot be saved at the exclusion of our private selves. Humanity, in terms of our personal identities, cannot be divided in such an artificial or mechanistic way that human nature proves to be fictitious. Whenever that does happen, the biblical concept of salvation, of wholeness, becomes a partial fiction in which pale ghosts of our full selves receive intangible and invisible credit slips designed to get us into heaven at some future date when we die. Heaven is not made less real or less important when the Bible insists on making God's salvation start here and now, in history and in time, with his gift of eternal life. Instead, a decision for Christ is changed from a minor and superficial choice to a major commitment which involves the wholeness of our humanity in private, social, and public dimensions of our being and is related to the wholeness of God's creation as the context of our existence. This creation itself is revealed as standing on tiptoe waiting for its release from bondage and decay and in throbbing expectancy and excitement awaits the redemption of the whole man.

The reality of heaven remains undiminished, but the reality of history looms larger as the place where our real decisions are made, where real relationships are formed, and where eternal destinies are to be decided and settled. What is needed, therefore, in our evangelistic concern and understanding is a person-to-person witness and approach which will reflect the biblical understanding of human nature and its needs, together with the biblical testimony of God's salvation with its wholeness. We do our fellow creatures no real service if we shortchange them from the full consciousness of Christian experience to which they are entitled in the gift of God through Jesus Christ. Nor can we ourselves, be fully faithful to the meaning of grace and the good news of the gospel if, for whatever the reason—tradition, blindness, or unwillingness to learn or grow—we refuse to move from old pictures and concepts in our heads which limit our ability to describe the lavishness of the salvation in Jesus Christ to which we are asked to bear our personal witness. The gospel means not only good news for the whole world, but it also means good news for the whole person!

5 | Picturing the New Person in Christ

We have been amplifying our understanding as to what it means to be a whole person in the light of the biblical account of creation and redemption. In that account, to be a living soul means that a person's material, bodily existence is filled with God's Spirit. A lost soul is a person whose unitary wholeness has been divided and shattered by willfulness, pride, and sin, separating him from his true life in God. This loss of integrity cannot be recovered by partial patching on either the inside or the outside of a person's life. Only the creative act of God in Jesus Christ can restore our "humpty-dumpty" brokenness so that we can experience the good news as a whole person and once again reflect our completeness in Christ. And, *that's* what it means to be a saved soul! Let us now picture the new person in Christ.

What we need to assist us in our person-to-person evangelistic witness is a new paradigm, a new picture, which more adequately reflects the biblical concepts of what it means to be a person in the contextual setting of the family, the community, the nation, the institutions and organizations which we establish and belong to, and the meaning of both our private and our public identities which emerge from our relationship to God and to nature. When Christ came in the fullness of times, the first century had to find a new vocabulary of expression to explain what was inexplicable and inexhaustible. New metaphors of meaning were demanded, and whenever Christ comes in any generation, old words strain because of their incapacity to contain or to exhaust the fullness of his being and of his meaning.

Despite our verbal inadequacies and inaccuracies, we must continue to probe and to be engaged in the task of providing new pictures which can faithfully reflect the content of our new life in Christ and the interior and extensive range of God's salvation. We know that when the Bible speaks of a new being in a new age, a person so new that the term "a new birth" is needed to explain his origins and his mystery, it must be describing more than "average" Christianity, wherein we ask each other to make a minimal commitment to Christ and a marginal commitment to his church. When we ask another person to sell all that he has to secure the pearl of great price, we must be asking for a different kind of radical decision than the mere signing of a card, or the raising of a hand, or walking down the aisle. Too many have assumed they could accept Christ while all of their old attachments remain intact, their old prejudices unchanged, their old value systems still operating, and their old lives very much the same as they were before, except for an hour or two on Sunday! When the Bible speaks about Christ's call to follow him, a profound personal transformation is involved, so that the new Christian believer feels that he is walking in a new world like a person who has just come back from death. Everything is changed in him and in his contextual relationships—far more than intellectual assent or superficial emotional feelings or volitional willingness.

How can we better describe this new reality? What new pictures can color the texture of our thinking, so that our minds can be transformed and we will be living in a new awareness of what it means when we ourselves are asked or when we invite another person to make a public decision of personal faith in Jesus Christ as Savior and Lord? Let us look at a picture which can begin to engage us in suggesting the dimensions of what it means to be fully human as a person and to experience the good news of God's salvation in its full intensity and power.

When we think about the vital dimensions of a person, we have grown accustomed to reporting the 36"-26"-36" measurements. Such facts may tell us something about the bodily proportions of a given person, but they are not the real dimensions of the whole being! To picture the full dimensions of personal existence, we are suggesting the following picture.[1]

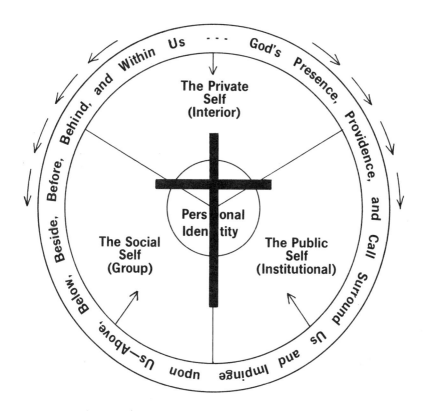

First, in looking at that picture, let me explain that there are two basic biblical assumptions so much a part of the illustration that they are not pictured. They are implicit, like a watermark in bond paper. The first assumption is founded on the biblical meaning of God's intention in his act of creation. Human persons are rooted in nature, even though sharing in God's image so that, like God himself, we are able to transcend (to stand over against—to be other than) nature. This truth enables us to find God and ourselves in nature, although nature is not capable of exhausting or explaining fully the richness of our personal being.

[1] Developed by the Evangelistic Life Style Program staff, Board of National Ministries, American Baptist Churches in the U.S.A.

The practical effect of this truth is that our personal identity must assume a bodily existence and a worldly existence. When we ask about the complexity of any person's life, we can only say that the mystery of our nature and destiny is rooted in our natural existence. Our humanity has a set of contextual givens which emerge from and relate us to the whole world of nature in which God's creative act establishes us. To be human means, in God's plan, a bodily existence in the world, which can be defined and described by the following terms: spiritual, social, sensory, temporal, spatial, material, sexual, mortal, historical, cultural, intellectual, creative, vocational, symbolical, accountable, existential, moral, paradoxical, psychological, physiological, emotional, rational, secular, political, ecological, mortal, and others!

There is a second biblical assumption in the new picture we are drawing which seeks to engage us in new awareness and understanding about essential identity and personhood. It is clear in the biblical narrative that the person is made by God to enjoy a personal relationship to him through the Spirit of Jesus Christ. The presence, providence, and the call of God surround, impinge upon, and penetrate into the circumference and marrow of our being. God's Spirit goes before us to lead and guide us, stays behind us to protect us, is above us to watch over us, is beneath us to support us, is beside us to befriend and help us, and is within us to enlighten and empower us.

The reconciling action of God in Jesus Christ and his cross is implicit to our Christian understanding of personal being. The cross of Christ, as the suffering love of God acting to complete what he first began in creation and to consummate the eternal purpose of his redemption, must be understood as standing at the center of the picture. Yet, its lines extend in all directions in unlimited scope. Unfortunately, no picture can adequately portray God without, at the same moment, falsifying aspects of his infinite being, much as it is impossible to represent the world as a sphere on the flat surface of a page of an atlas. When we picture God as the impinging presence on the entire circumference of our human existence, we seem to falsify the fact that he is also at the very center. To picture God there, at the center, and to draw an inner circle, would ignore his presence and claim at the circumference. We can only say that God is not just at the center; he is the center. He is not only just at the circumference or in part of its arc; he is the circumference. Whatever the angle of the arc, God is fully present in all the dimensions of our existence. No part of our lives is meant to be lived outside of his presence. No need, therefore, common to humanity, is beyond his understanding care; and no relationships can exist in health and wholeness independent of God and the context of our personal identity and integrity.

To be a whole person is to know that God's original concern (Acts 15:14, Moffatt) has been restored in Jesus Christ. Originally God made us for himself, but we sinned and suffered alienation from him and made ourselves as strangers and enemies. Originally God made us to enjoy an honest self-respect and self-esteem emerging from our ability to love ourselves in the right way and for the right reasons. But our sin marred the image of God in us, and we find ourselves living with disfigured faces in self-contempt, often unrecognizable in our efforts to buy or to win social approval with which we can justify ourselves. As a result, we suffer self-alienation, and no longer at home to our private self, we live in the bondage of sin, death, and anxious dread. Jesus pictures this awful inner emptiness in his story of the person's house swept clean of all its demons. But its emptiness is filled again so that the last estate is far worse than the first. God's original concern was that the person would be a full member of the human family and of a good society where love and justice—two sides of interdependent relationships—would serve as legal tender in the currency of the realm. But, like the two sons in the story in Luke 15, we have suffered alienation from the family and from its larger society expressed in social groups. Some of us have taken our share of the family estate and have used up these assets in selfish prodigality. Others think they are maintaining a closer physical relationship in the Father's house, but it turns out that (psychologically and socially) like the elder brother, distance and social alienation are all the more angry and intense. As the record tells us, the elder brother "was angry and refused to go in" (Luke 15:28).

God's original concern was for us to enjoy our membership in history as builders of cities and culture, with their richness of the aesthetic arts and their variety of institutional form and organizational structure designed to serve the common good. Here in the public realm, a person's private and social life was meant to take shape and form so that temporal deeds could be expressed and then conserved for unborn generations. Sinning against God meant not only sinning against ourselves and the human family gathered in society, but it also meant sinning against the common good and investing our public life and their institutions of culture, of commerce, of education, of business, and of government with the demonic product of our personal alienation. While we are busy building our towers of Babel, we leave no ungleaned fields for the poor. Failing either to give love or justice, we profit from their poverty, and, as Amos, the prophet, warned, we buy the poor for a pair of shoes. (See Amos 8:6.)

Asserting ourselves in willful pride, manipulating nature as we strip its resources of minerals, ores, and oxygen to build our economy and its supporting political institutions, we have seen our public structures and institutions tend to become dehumanizing instruments of social change. As they increase in size, no single hand is able to steer or to control their momentum and direction so that often they proceed with their own speed and force and in their own direction, despite the protests of converted Christian men, who, as individuals, try to get a hand on the steering wheel. As Winston Churchill observed, "First we shape and build our institutions and next we discover that they are shaping and mastering us."

What is greatly missed in much of our evangelistic witness today is the good news of the biblical doctrine of humanity which describes our personal being as God intended it to be in his first creation. What we miss in much of our understanding of the gospel is the good news of how God has acted in Jesus Christ with cosmic force and power to unseat the demonic aspects of human life and to win a cosmic victory so that the gospel can become good news for the whole person. What we miss is the biblical understanding of creation and of salvation which makes the gospel good news and assists us in understanding our personal identity, not in the separate parts and splinters and shavings of the person, but in terms of our private and social and public realities.

The picture we have sought to offer will be improved upon and enriched as we are engaged together in study, action, and dialogue. But the picture will encourage us to start the pilgrimage with the assurance that our further explorations will not yield a fruitless search. God's intent in creation means that our personal identities will be understood, not in terms of the private and interior self alone, but also in terms of our social selves and our public and institutional selves. The dimensions of this identity will be seen as full and equal partners enabling us not only to know ourselves as we are outside of Christ, segmented and divided, but also to know ourselves as we are destined to be in Christ, complete and integrated.

In extending the invitation to our friends and neighbors to trust Jesus Christ and to receive the gift of God's salvation, we must make it clear that the private self is not the whole person. Nor is social self the whole person. No public self or image is the whole person. Religious man (or woman), economic man, businessman, music man, space man, married man, spiritual man, political man, public man— these are but the partial shavings of the whole, and often they describe functions more than our essential being. God's original intention in creation which was spoiled by our sin and its alienation has been fulfilled in the work of Christ. In redemption, God acts to complete what sin has interrupted, to restore what our human alienation has destroyed, and to consummate his own purposes which existed from the foundation of the ages. In redemption, God has acted to take the brokenness of our human existence and to make it whole again.

God's salvation intends wholeness, the recovery of true identity in Jesus Christ so that our personal being is set free to receive and to realize the full dimensions offered to us in the new age. To offer our friends a private salvation while their social and public existence remains unclaimed or unchanged by Christ is only to increase the divisions within their being which already exist and to make their sense of estrangement more intolerable. But, to know what a person is in terms of what he may become in Christ enables us to engage in person-to-person witness, not on a marginal or superficial level, but on the deepest level of interpersonal meaning where deep calls unto deep. To understand the mystery and the wholeness of our personal being, together with the wholeness of God's salvation, enables personal evangelism to be for us what God intended it to be when he acted in Jesus Christ to reconcile the whole world to himself and to redeem the whole person to himself.

Our personal witness, then, is a testimony to the objective realities which exist because of what Christ is and what he has already done in our behalf. More than that, our personal witness is a call for all those who hear the good news to respond with personal faith and to make a public commitment of themselves to a new style of life wherein they can more faithfully fulfill God's call. These profound transformations in our private, our social, and our public aspects of being contribute to what the New Testament declares is a brand-new creation in Jesus Christ. That new creation, living in Christ and in community, manifests itself in what we have chosen to call "an evangelistic life style."

Let us acknowledge God's call daily and, by his grace and help, covenant together to live with integrity, as we accept God's help in pardon and forgiveness and freedom, which gets our "humpty-dumpty" brokenness all together. Second, we accept our destiny in his family to live interdependently with love and justice expressed to those not only in the household of faith but also to all persons everywhere as members of a new community, created and sustained by God's presence and Spirit. Third, we commit ourselves to accept the unfinished stewardship given to us at the first creation to build up the earth and to conserve its resources for the generations to come, remembering that the earth is the Lord's and the fullness thereof. This covenant commitment on our part will enable us to announce everywhere that the gospel is indeed good news to the whole person.

6 | The Evangelistic Life Style of Good News People

At the beginning of our study together, we looked briefly at the paradox in our personal situations. We observed that God made the world good; we have remade it bad. God made us as persons in his own image. We have broken the image and alienated ourselves from the Lord. Because we live in darkness instead of the reflected radiance of God's light, we have lost our own identity and our personal integrity. In turn, our human divisions have shattered the human community of interdependence intended by God. In our efforts to hide ourselves, we seek shelter in temporary groups formed upon false foundations, and, as we live in pride asserting our independence, we sin against our neighbor and our world. Our sin against neighbor includes injustice and inequity, and our sin against the world takes the form of selfish exploitation. We abuse the earth and radically alter the support systems that would keep our planet green and growing and our human lives livable. An evangelistic life style will commit us to accept the forgiveness of our sin in Jesus Christ as our Savior. An evangelistic life style will be our decision to accept his lordship over all of life. To be in Christ and to be called to live with God's people as a colony of heaven on earth will mean a recovery of personal identity and integrity as God's saving action unites in one person our private, our public, and our social selves. To be in Christ will mean a recovery of interdependence as we live as members of the Christian community where we are members one of another. To be in Christ will mean a recovery of the original stewardship task entrusted to us at the first creation when God asked us to dress the garden and to keep it and thus to act as his agents in building up the earth.

To accept God's redemption in its cosmic intention and to receive his salvation as wholeness will involve us in a new outlook and in a brand-new life as we follow Christ and his way. In that basic commitment and stance, we want now to interpret additional criteria which can serve as distinguishing marks of our evangelistic life style. There are seven identifying "marks" which can be used to characterize the evangelistic life style of persons engaged in Christian witness. Those seven marks are like brand marks. They identify to whom we belong and what the nature of our business is as Christians. They include: (1) affirmation, (2) repentance, (3) proclamation, (4) invitation, (5) celebration, (6) commitment, and (7) sacrifice.[1] We want now to look briefly at each of these distinguishing traits as criteria which can further describe the evangelistic life style embraced by "good news people."

1. *Affirmation* means accepting God's forgiveness for our sins and his saving presence and power in our lives. In his letter to Corinth, the apostle Paul writes, "all the promises of God find their Yes in him" (2 Corinthians 1:20). Because Jesus lives forever, he continues as God's pledge of personal pardon, and the new and living Way which he has opened into the heart of God remains accessible to us (Hebrews 10:19-21). We can be sure of our life in Christ, because it is God himself who places his mark of ownership upon us and who gives us the Holy Spirit in our hearts as the guarantee of all that he has for us (2 Corinthians 1:21-22). The "yes" which Jesus brings is an affirmation of God's original intention for us in creation, leading to the restoration of broken relationships and meanings. God's "yes" in Christ is a "yes" to our human existence, so that to be saved is not to be saved *from* but *for* our new humanity in Christ. The "yes" which we see affirmed in Jesus is a "yes" to liberation, which forever frees us from the need to scapegoat others for our faults and sins. Christ's forgiveness assures us that our past failures need not be final. His "yes" means a "yes" to a new future and to a new confirming Christian fellowship. His affirmation is a "yes" to life and a new way to use life, which we see reflected in his own ministry.

The New Testament makes it very plain that God's love for us is unconditionally affirming and accepting. Of course, this does not mean that he is always pleased with, or that he approves of, all our motives or actions. But while we were yet sinners, helpless, Christ died for us commending God's love to us. In that love, we see his

[1] These seven marks were identified by the Evangelism Team of the Board of National Ministries, American Baptist Churches in the U.S.A.

method of redemption. Throughout the New Testament, as in the entire Bible, God is revealed acting in grace and mercy as one who is for us an advocate and a believing friend.

Some time ago, I had a phone call from a friend in trouble in a neighborhood bar. Some months before he had "fallen off the wagon" and was now drinking himself to death. He told me over the phone, "I have no money and nowhere to go tonight. Will you help me?" I was busy and my evening was already planned. But I responded and said, "Stay there, and I'll come by to pick you up." Later, when I walked into the dimly lit bar, I found it reeking with stale beer and tobacco smoke. I saw my friend dejectedly seated on a bar stool, all of his friends gone, like the wind, with his money. Since that occasion, he has turned a personal corner and has come a long way back to a meaningful life of social usefulness and a newfound feeling of healthy self-respect. He explains his comeback from hopelessness and despair as God's work of divine grace. He believes that God acted in his circumstances to forgive him and to give him a new life with a new future. How can he believe that? "Because," as he says in partial explanation, "other people were willing to believe in me, even when my life had little in it to make my future redemption believable." We are sure that good news people are meant by God to be those characterized by constructive attitudes of acceptance and affirmation instead of negative and destructive feelings and actions of rejection and condemnation. In relating to other people, good news people will seek to embody the "yes" of Jesus in thought and action, remembering that he came not to condemn the world, but to save the world (John 3:17). One of the greatest affirming words in the entire Bible may be found when Jesus says to Simon Peter, "I have prayed for you" (Luke 22:31). That's where affirmation must begin, and that's where it often will end.

2. *Repentance* is a decision which leads us to a new outlook. We face an entirely new direction and live in a new way. Repentance starts in our mind's eye, so that the metaphors by which we understood ourselves in the past as imprisoned can be changed and new metaphors can open possibilities of significant transformations, bridging the distance between what we are and what God intends us to be.

Other English words, like metabolism and metamorphosis, help us to see what the Greek New Testament word for repentance, *metanoia,* signifies. Metabolism speaks of our basic physiological system and the chemical changes which may take place in our bodies. Metamorphosis means a change of shape. *Metanoia* means a change of mind. The first part of these words, *meta*, is derived from *mita*, meaning a conical column marking a turning point in a race in the Roman circus. Repentance is the turning point in life where our personal decision for Christ turns us around and we experience God's transforming love for ourselves. A New English Bible translation of 2 Timothy 2:25 illustrates repentance with these words: "The Lord may grant them a change of heart and show them the truth, and thus they may come to their senses. . . ."

Good news people are people who themselves have responded to God's confirming action in Christ by personal repentance. In turn, as they relate to others, they live with a prayer that God may show others the truth also, which will lead them to a change of heart and bring them to their senses. In the story of the prodigal son, "to come to your senses" was the moment of truth out in the far country when the younger son saw what his father was like and what he, himself, was like. When he came to himself, the Bible says, he made his decision to arise and go to his father. Repentance, therefore, is not just a mental exercise; it leads to measurable differences and directions in our actions.

Repentance is the decision and the process which enables us to discover that the grace of God proves greater than all our sin and leads us to new beginnings. Good news people know that, and they live in the midst of hopelessness as people of hope to whom God has opened up a new future.

3. *Proclamation* means announcing the mighty truths and acts of God to everyone, everywhere, in all the settings of our lives. There are many ways in which this may be done. Good news people keep themselves sensitive and alert, so that in airplanes and automobiles, on the job or on the golf course, in their neighborhoods or at school, they will find openings where the good news can be honestly shared. The earlier chapters of this book discussed the meaning of the good news message, so that little new needs to be said at this point. Perhaps we could let three New Testament passages summarize the characteristics of proclamation. (*a*) John 20:31 tells us the Bible was written to announce the good news of salvation, as completed in Christ, thereby satisfying the hunger of the human heart. (*b*) 1 John 5:13-14 tells us that the good news of salvation brings confidence in Christ, thereby stabilizing our precarious lives. (*c*) Romans 15:4 reminds us that the Bible was written to announce the good news of salvation as comfort and hope in Christ, thereby strengthening our discouraged souls.

In Colossians 4:10-11, Paul speaks of three Christian friends as a comfort to him. Good news people prove to be such a comfort and fragrance wherever they are found, assuaging pain while encouraging and nurturing the best hopes of friends and neighbors in the proclamation of the Christian faith.

4. *Invitation* means calling forth the faithful responses of our friends and neighbors and loved ones in the family circle to accept the adequacy of Jesus Christ, to free us from the limitations of a binding past, and to call forth our undeveloped gifts for his service and our stewardship. The invitation which we extend is the extension of Christ's own invitation to us and through us to others: "Come and see." "Seek and find." "Knock and doors will open." "Taste and see." His invitation is extended to everyone without reservation. No one is too good not to need it, and no one is too bad to be beyond the reach of his voice. The epistle of Peter tells us that Christ preached to the spirits in prison (1 Peter 3:18-20). Later, the Apostles' Creed interprets this to mean that, after his death and burial, before his resurrection, "He descended into hell." Such a declaration represents the efforts of the early church to understand and to affirm the staggering good news of how extensive the gospel invitation is in Jesus Christ. Nothing is to be regarded "off limits" to his limitless love. If the gates of hell cannot stand against his church, weak and divided as it often is, we should not be surprised to learn that the gates of hell have been breached by the love of Christ, strong Son of God, acting for persons in their behalf and for their plenteous redemption.

Another minister has explained the meaning of God's invitation in Jesus Christ. He had helped a young man who had drifted away into a life of rebellion and then crime. The minister had visited him in prison and encouraged him to accept the truth of God's acceptance of him in Christ and to take steps to complete his formal schooling while serving his sentence. Some time later, the young man wrote from his prison cell to thank the pastor for his friendship and help. In part, he said, "You were my last chance. When I felt like giving up, I kept going on because of your confidence in me." In replying, the pastor wrote, "I preach a gospel of what God has done for all of us in Christ. I want you to know that I believe with all my heart that God has acted in Christ for you. On that confidence and faith, I am willing to bet my life."

To read an exchange like that is to recognize that God's invitation and ours are closely allied to affirmation. Invitation is the way Jesus relates to others, and it is the mark which we as Christians will want to wear also to identify ourselves as "good news people" with a distinctive evangelistic life style.

5. *Celebration* expresses a sense of joy and gladness in the whole creation of God, rejoicing that the earth is the Lord's and the fullness thereof, while affirming the sacramental beauty of nature which reveals the glory and greatness of God. Celebration means also a new blessedness and hope because of the good news we have heard and by which we live. It is understandable why Christians speak of celebrating Christmas, Good Friday, Easter, and similar events as a

part of their religious festival and the victory of faith. These events teach us the meaning of our human life and our relationship to nature and to the world. Nowhere does this appear with more pertinence than in the human life of Jesus himself. Some people expected Jesus to be a religious recluse, rejecting the meaning of his personal and social existence, denying the reality of his manhood and its bodily nature and needs. Others expected Jesus to be a religious ascetic, retreating and withdrawing from the natural life. All were shocked and disappointed by his behavior. He attended weddings and enjoyed their celebration; he ate and drank, so that his critics called him "a winebibber and glutton."

When the Bible tells us that Jesus, the Word, became flesh, it helps to correct those who believed that evil was rooted in the human body or in bodily nature. We are reminded that God himself has fashioned the material aspects of our bodily existence as human beings. The Bible says that everything which God has made is good, not only because of his original, creative act; but also because in redemption, it may be consecrated by the Word of God and by prayer. Such an affirmation, illustrated in the life of Jesus, reminds us that God made all the organs and glands of our bodies. He gives us our appetites, as well as our aspirations. The human life of Jesus helps us to celebrate our whole human lives as Christians, which includes our material relationships and the social settings of our bodily existence.

As good news people, we can celebrate in the life of the church and in the life of the world all that God has done in his creation and in his redemption to give us tidings of great joy for all the people. One should not forget the description which Jesus made of the joy in heaven over the recovery of that which is lost when it is found. And, in the same way, the story in Luke 15 can never really be understood or appreciated unless we make room for the music and the dancing with which the return of the prodigal was celebrated in the father's house.

6. *Commitment* means not only to give ourselves to Jesus Christ in a private decision of faith, but also to profess him publicly as Lord and Savior, to accept believer's baptism as ordination to his fellowship and service. Our original commitment must lead to new decisions as we grow in our understanding and in our faith. Commitment means the ability to pledge ourselves to a continuing partnership with Jesus Christ and his people to work and witness at those points and in those places where we ourselves as persons and the society to which we belong need changing and transformation. Christian commitment begins with a decision to surrender all that we know about ourselves to all that we know about Jesus Christ. That includes a decision to believe, to belong, and to become. It would include continuing commitments to follow Christ day by day; to be in fellowship with his people; to further the concerns of love and justice for which Jesus lived, died, and rose again; and to abandon the false fictions by which we sought to live. We are called to live before the face of God so that our features may be conformed to his likeness and to become fruit-bearing branches, whose leaves shall be for the healing of the nations.

When the late William Temple was Archbishop of Canterbury, he published a summary of findings on the place and witness of Christians in today's world. Basically, his document, which he entitled *What Christians Stand for in the Secular World,*[2] dealt with the meaning of Christian commitment. He identified five basic decisions which he saw as a visible part of a person's commitment to Christ as Savior and Lord. They included: (1) A decision for God who has spoken, revealing his will for justice and righteousness in the vast world of personal relationships and giving us a pattern to follow in the life of his own Son. (2) A decision for our neighbor, near at hand and far away, the neighbor whom God has given us to love and to serve. (3) A decision for man as rooted in nature. Neglect of this decision leads us to exploit the world and to ignore our interdependence both in it and with it. (4) A decision for history, where the meaning of God's work and ways is revealed and actualized. (5) A decision for the gospel and the church. While we face the need to cooperate with all who are pursuing aims in accord with God's intended purpose for man's temporal life, Temple saw that our commitment to Christ means a continuing commitment to his church, despite its weakness and imperfections. Good news people will carry these marks of decision and commitment wherever they go.

7. *Sacrifice* means an honest recognition that God's call in Christ involves the risk of relationship and response. We hear the call to take up his cross as an instrument of redemptive love, and we face this challenge to accept the risk of sharing in his ministry of reconciling action with its opportunities for struggle and for conflict (2 Corinthians 5:18-19).

Christian people often are asked to pray for the salvation of the world. Good news people will recognize that such a prayer, unless it is vain and empty, will mean measurable changes in the way that people in the world think and live. Whenever Christianity has gone into an alien culture, it brings about radical transformations to that way of life and to its society as well. Human sacrifice, infanticide, and cannibalism could not live long in the light of Christ and the value which he shed on human life. Slavery in America was abolished and child labor legislation was enacted largely because Christian people accepted the risk of sacrifice in following Christ as Lord of life as well as a private Savior.

In the New Testament when the apostolic party came to Ephesus, a city-wide riot broke out, sponsored by silversmiths who saw that

---

[2] William Temple, *What Christians Stand for in the Secular World* (Philadelphia: Fortress Press, n.d.).

Jesus and the Christian way of life were a substantial threat to their profitable craft of idol making. Christians in Ephesus faced the risk of sacrifice as they had done earlier when magicians brought their books of magic and burned them publicly, thereby signifying their clean break with their old way of life. The cross is at the heart of our Christian worship because it is at the heart of our Christian faith and discipleship. Good news people are willing to carry the cross as they learn to use life in a new way.

Arthur John Gossip has an eloquently poignant passage in which he reminds us that the life of Christ remains for all time the revelation as to how life is meant to be lived—heights it can rise to and lengths it is willing to go—so that we come to feel that to use life on other terms than his is to be guilty of some form of embezzlement. Calvary speaks of sacrifice, not because it seeks blamelessness, but because it shows that in the center of God's heart there is a holy passion and a suffering love. No evil motive is ascribed to Dives or to the priest or to the Levite in the stories told by Jesus. But they took no notice! To them, and to others, like the rich young ruler and to many of us—Dr. Gossip hears the Lord saying: "You are doing nothing with life except trying to keep it clean. You are here to be used . . . life is to be spent and given."[3] Sacrifice is symbolized in the prodigal extravagance of the woman who anointed Jesus with her cask of precious ointment. "Wherever this gospel will be preached," Jesus tells us, "her memorial will be celebrated." (See Matthew 26:13.) Why? Because, among the leaders and teachers, she most nearly understood the heart of God and his lavish way of self-giving and sacrifice! That's the good news of witness we can share. If God spared not his own Son, we can believe that, with him, he will freely give us all that we need!

These seven marks do not tell us everything about what good news people are meant to be like. But they can provide some distinguishable traits. As we engage in the task of person-to-person witness, they may serve also as criteria to help us answer the questions: "What are you asking me to commit myself to, as a new follower of Jesus Christ?" or "What does it mean to believe in Jesus Christ and to make a public profession of him as my Lord and Savior?" To these questions, we can say: "To be a 'good news person' in Christ means to adopt an evangelistic life style characterized by affirmation—repentance—proclamation—invitation—celebration—commitment—sacrifice!"

[3] Arthur John Gossip, *Experience Worketh Hope* (New York: Charles Scribner's Sons, 1945), pp. 42-52.

7 | Models for a Person-to-Person Witness

Evangelism has been one of the major thrusts of the Protestant churches in America. Early in our national history, churches began to send missionaries overseas where they worked with the people there to win others to Christ and to establish churches. The story of westward expansion in this country is not complete without the accounts of the revivals and planting of churches on the ever-moving frontier. In the urban areas, as people crowded in to take jobs in the burgeoning industries, the churches adapted their programs to meet the need. Bilingual churches were established so that immigrants could worship God and find Christ even though they had not yet learned a new language. In the South after the Civil War, the churches were among the first groups to provide educational opportunities for the black people who had newly gained their freedom. At the same time, education enabled the black churches to launch a renewed evangelistic emphasis.

Theological controversies which erupted in the first half of this century interrupted the evangelistic spirit and ministry in many of the churches. Fruitless debates and discussions replaced a willingness to be involved personally in making Christ known winsomely and contagiously. As a result, the passion for evangelism was chilled and its spirit dampened. Many developed a "wait and see" attitude. Some waited for church buildings to evangelize our communities and neighborhoods. My own pastorate in Detroit is now related to a congregation which has been housed in an unusually beautiful sanctuary and educational facilities. But since 1958 we have averaged only twenty-eight baptisms per year. Our building could not be a more eloquent statement in stone, but our congregation has discovered that buildings cannot evangelize.

Many others of the laity have been waiting for a superior breed of minister who might appear to win the whole world for Christ. Others have made an unconscious conclusion that the evangelistic task resides in persons and organizations, such as the Billy Graham Evangelistic Association, Oral Roberts, or similar "impact" agencies. Still others have been waiting for the denominational headquarters' staff to do our work in evangelism. Finally, it appears that most of us have made a discovery. The most effective method of evangelism is found in the New Testament models which we see in the ministry and conversation of Jesus and in the life of the early church. Andrew first found his own brother, Simon, and brought him to Jesus. Philip found Nathaniel and told him, "We have found the Messiah." The woman of Samaria returned from her conversation with Jesus and told the whole city. The person-to-person, face-to-face witness has never been superseded as the most effective way for Christian people to share their faith so that God's Spirit can summon others to a personal decision for Jesus Christ and his church. In recognizing these facts, we want now to look at several passages of the New Testament which can provide us some learning models to help shape the structures and style of our own person-to-person witness. These models can assist us in answering our questions: "How can we tell the Good News most effectively and naturally in the places where we live and work? How can we become a 'good news person'?"

First, we shall examine several representative situations to let them state their own facts. Later, we shall draw some conclusions which may serve as formative suggestions for our current experience today.

Luke 10. In this narrative, we find a summary of Jesus sending out the seventy. (For the sake of the record, we might note that later manuscripts have identified the traditional seventy as seventy-two.) In reading the textual account, twelve essential facts stand out and are easily identified. (1) These persons were chosen and appointed for their mission. (2) They were commissioned and sent ahead of Jesus to announce his presence and kingdom. (3) They went two-by-two, thereby deriving strength from their mutual participation. (4) They were laymen (the same astonishing fact emerges in Acts 4:13, where we are informed that the members of the council were amazed to see the boldness of Peter and John and to learn that they were ordinary men without the rabbinic education deemed necessary to be a teacher. One of the words used is *idiotes,* from which we get our

English words "idiom" or "idiot." This signified a private person or a nonprofessional. Early in the ministry of Jesus, the priesthood of all believers emerged as a substantial fact). (5) They were encouraged to pray for allies and reinforcements. (6) They were given resources more than adequate for their task in the presence of God's Spirit. (7) They had a message of conciliation, rather than condemnation: "Peace be to this house." (8) They were encouraged to establish the language of relationship by staying in one house. (9) They were to announce that the kingdom of God had come near in Jesus Christ. (10) Their message also announced the serious and sobering fact of personal accountability before the judgment of God. (11) They returned from their mission with a joy of accomplishment. (12) The power of their witness was not in what they said, but in the power and victory of Jesus' name.

Acts 8. In this passage, we read the account of Philip's witness to the Ethiopian official, returning from Jerusalem where he had been at worship. We note the following facts: (1) There was a divine call, which Philip received, "Get ready and go." (2) There was a human response, "Philip got ready and went." (3) There were unsearchable resources at work—the Holy Spirit sees and guides, both the seeker and the sought. (4) There was a meeting at the right moment, the opportune time in the providence of God. (5) There was a dialogical relationship which was established, involving closeness (verse 29), listening (verse 30), questioning (verse 30), invitation (verse 31), and acceptance (verse 31). (6) There was the powerful witness and use of the Scriptures. (7) There was a teachable moment of searching inquiry and questioning. (8) There was the wisdom of the teacher, who began where the person was. (9) There was a shared witness, focusing in the good news about Jesus. (10) There was a personal decision of faith, which culminated in a public acknowledgment of Christ as Lord and Savior, confirmed in the experience of believer's baptism leading to great joy and continued usefulness.

Luke 19:1-10. In this brief narrative, we read about the conversation of Jesus which led to the conversion of Zacchaeus. We note: (1) There was a sense of urgent excitement as Jesus passed through Jericho. There were the crowds, and there was Zacchaeus running. (2) There was the past history of Jericho, related to the biography of the city. Rahab, the harlot, lived in Jericho (Joshua 2:1-21). Joshua's battle for Jericho was part of its spiritual saga. Mark Antony gave Jericho to Cleopatra, and Zacchaeus was now in Jericho as its chief tax collector. (3) In that office, he was trapped by the stereotyped expectations of the community and assigned a fixed role and status from which there appeared to be no escape. (4) Zacchaeus was also trapped by the misdeeds of his own past life. Fraud and corruption had been related to his office. (5) Zacchaeus was inspired to outrun the limits of his past and all of the stereotyped aspects present in his situation. (6) Jesus identified him by his own name, related to him as a real person, broke the stereotypes, and accepted the reality of his personhood manifested by eating at his table. (7) Jesus announced God's salvation as revealed in the decision and commitment of Zacchaeus. (8) Jesus explained his mission to the "outsider": "The Son of Man has come to seek and to save that which is lost." (9) Zacchaeus was led to make a radical break with his past. (10) And he restored fourfold in a new style of life involving restitution and the stewardship of honest responsibility.

Luke 15. In these three familiar parables, we see examples of evangelistic attitudes and relationships, which constantly renew themselves in meaning and in power. (1) We discover that the evangelistic spirit involves a search for that which is lost. (2) Looking for the lost implies seeing. The father was able to see his son while he was yet a great way off. Love is not blind, but love is bound to the other person. (3) Looking implies flexibility of method. One does not look for the lost coin in the same way or in the same place as one does for the lost sheep or the lost sons. For the lost coin, you light the lamp and you narrow the focus of your search; for the lost sheep, you leave the house and the sheepfold to widen and extend your search; for your lost boy, your prayers run out into the far country together with your hopes. (4) Looking also involves a long and faithful persistence; you look and look until your search is rewarded and the lost has been found. (5) Looking also involves listening. How does a sheep tell you it is lost? It is missed, but one also may know by its forlorn bleating. How does a coin tell you it is lost? By its absence from your pocket, or by its ability to speak, glinting in the light or ringing when dislodged. How does a son tell you he is lost? By his absence and his alienation. (6) Next, looking also demands love. Love offers acceptance in the place of alienation, grace in the place of guilt, confirmation in the place of censure and condemnation. We see two conflicting attitudes, that expressed in the father and that in the elder brother. Instinctively, we perceive what might have happened to us, when timidly we responded, if we had been met by the elder brother in this story.

You are invited to continue your own examination and study of Jesus' conversations in calling his first disciples (John 1:35-51); with Nicodemus (John 3:1-17); with the woman of Samaria (John 4:5-42); with the long-time impotent man at Bethesda's pool (John 5:1-17);

with the woman taken in adultery (John 8:2-11, KJV); and with the man born blind (John 9:1-38). To look at the record of these conversations will be to discover some clear examples which can serve as formative models for our own person-to-person style of evangelistic witness. Some conclusions leap out to us.

First, we note the refusal of Jesus to stereotype the people whom he meets. In one of his essays, W. H. Auden notes the tendency which people have to caricature and stereotype other people. He describes a caricature or stereotype as a frozen face which assigns to its owner a fixed and rigid past but denies to him any possibility of change in the future. We pick out the worst examples in definable groups and categories, and we make that small selection represent the entire group. For example, we know a few Baptists and they have impressed us as "ugly bigots." On the basis of that small knowledge, we stereotype all Baptists as bigots. We know a lawyer who was disbarred from his profession and we stereotype all lawyers as "shysters" and "crooks." We learn about a doctor who turns out to be a "quack" and we stereotype all doctors as "quacks."

And what we do with the professions, we do with ethnic groups more readily. Here we come into our stereotypes which picture Scottish people as "tightwads"; black people as "shiftless"; Polish people as "stupid"; Italian people as "sensualists"; Jewish people as "agnostics" or "Christ-killers." On the basis of our stereotypes, we lump and dump whole groups of people into a common mold which seems to justify our fears and our lack of real relationship. We discover that Jesus' method is just the opposite from our tendency to stereotype people by groups or categories. Each person has a name, his or her own reality of existence, needs, and questions, and Jesus relates to each person on the basis of who he or she is and where he or she is standing.

Secondly, Jesus is prompted by love to find a common ground with other people. I remember a report, made by the Johns Hopkins Foundation in Baltimore. It involved a study of twenty young men who appeared to be well on their way to lives of criminal behavior, of becoming social dropouts. Mysteriously, the paths of these twenty young men had veered from the road of their social delinquency. Upon investigation, the team discovered there was a single schoolteacher who had had profound influence and impact on each of these twenty young men. In retirement, she was interviewed by members of the research team. When she was asked about these students by name, she said, "Yes, I remember all of these young men very well; I loved each one of them."

The capacity to love penetrates into the innermost recesses of our personal being. It is the capacity of love, which gets behind the apparent facts about ourselves and brings into a luminous light the possibilities which are resident in all of us as persons. The facts are so often limiting, damning, and indicting. But love penetrates beyond these superficial barriers because there is no end to its trust, no limit

to its endurance, no fading of its hope; love never fails. So the method of Jesus was to look through all of the limiting factors of a person's past, or one's present expectations. He enables a person to see for the first time what the future might become.

In thinking about our need to establish a common ground with the other persons with whom we may become related in the language of love and relationship, one is surprised to see this same dimension emerge in the apostle Paul. Our superficial conclusions about him as a person lead us to see him as an authoritarian, dogmatic individual; but listen to him in his letter to the Corinthians:

"I have freely and happily become a servant of any and all so that I can win them to Christ. When I am with the Jews I seem as one of them so that they will listen to the Gospel and I can win them to

Christ. When I am with Gentiles who follow Jewish customs and ceremonies I don't argue, even though I don't agree, because I want to help them. When with the heathen I agree with them as much as I can, except of course that I must always do what is right as a Christian. And so, by agreeing, I can win their confidence and help them too.

"When I am with those whose consciences bother them easily, I don't act as though I know it all and don't say they are foolish; the result is that they are willing to let me help them. Yes, whatever a person is like, I try to find common ground with him so that he will let me tell him about Christ and let Christ save him" (1 Corinthians 9:19b-22, *The Living Bible*).

In the third place, the refusal to stereotype and force people into damning structures of our own judgment, together with the capacity to establish a language of relationship and love and to find common ground as a meeting place, enables people to abandon their old scripts and to embrace a new redemptive role. For example, Eric Berne has reported his observations that most of us as adults act in ways that seem as if they have been predetermined. He sees us as actors on a stage, reading a script prepared for us by our parents or by other influential people from our past. This script has cast us in certain roles and relationships so that we find ourselves on stage repeating the lines and acting out the parts in which we have been cast. Often we discover that we have been miscast and that we are thereby miscasting ourselves. As a result, we not only do not like the play or the producers; but also it turns out that we can't like ourselves.[1] Not feeling OK about myself, it is difficult for me to feel OK about other people in my own church or in other churches. If I really can't accept myself as a Baptist, I may find it hard to accept Methodists and Presbyterians and Roman Catholics and Jews. If I can't accept and be at home in my own culture, then I may find it difficult to accept people from other cultures. If my life's script dictates a feeling that I'm not OK, that may often lead to "a you're not OK" action and a rejection of others. And, if I do not act destructively against you, I may find it necessary to act destructively in some ways against myself so that I cannot establish a loving relationship with others. If I can't love myself with the proper kind of self-regard and self-esteem, it will be impossible for me to love either my neighbor or my brother as I love myself.

In the fourth place, Jesus, in his method of conversation,

---

[1] Muriel James and Dorothy Jongeward, *Born to Win* (Reading, Mass.: Addison-Wesley Publishing Co., Inc., 1973), pp. 68-100. See also Thomas A. Harris, *I'm Ok— You're OK* (New York: Harper & Row, Publishers, 1969), chap. 3.

established a dialogical method as his main style in person-to-person relationships. A monologue sees us preaching, performing, and talking, and the other person becomes only a listener who must find ways to defend himself against the barrage of our attacking words. But Jesus starts where the person is. He accepts the person as he or she is. He accepts one's right to exist, one's right to have one's own name, one's right to have one's past—good or bad—one's right to have one's own questions, one's right to ask questions. So Jesus is able to pierce many of the meaning barriers which are created by defensiveness, by fear, and by resistance.

In his book, *The Miracle of Dialogue,* Reuel Howe speaks about five barriers which get in the way of meaning and prevent understanding in our communication. *Words* have a different value dependent upon their emotional content in our past experience. In the same way, two people may carry different *pictures* in their heads about each other. *Defenses* and *anxieties* block the possibility of honest dialogue and thwart our seeing and hearing the other person's vantage point and point of view. *Crossed purposes* are conflicting goals which serve to thwart a common meeting of meaning.[2] Our task as person-to-person witnesses is to build bridges, not barriers. A willingness to come out from behind our own defenses and to run the risk of honest relationship will encourage others to come out from behind their barricades and to find a common meeting ground.

Another fact which emerges as a conclusion is that Jesus has refused to mechanize God's methods of dealing with and reaching people or to canonize one of his own methods. In his conversation with Nicodemus, he speaks about the mysteries of the way in which God works. He that is born of the Spirit is like the wind. One does not know from whence the wind comes and whither it is blowing, but one sees the effects of it. Jesus is reminding his hearers that no person is able to manipulate the wind. We do not manage it or control it. So, in our person-to-person evangelistic methods, we must resist the temptation to canonize one pattern or one procedure as though this is the way God must always work. We must resist our temptation to find security behind the safe methods of the past.

In this connection, it is interesting to note in the book of Acts what the record says about how the Spirit is given to Christian believers. In the eighth chapter, we discover that the Holy Spirit is given *after* baptism. In the tenth chapter, we discover that the Spirit is given

---

[2] Reuel L. Howe, *The Miracle of Dialogue* (New York: The Seabury Press, Inc., 1963), pp. 18-35.

before baptism. In Acts 19, we find the Spirit given *in* baptism. It is as though God deliberately is helping the young church to discover that no denomination and no religious practice should be based on any one method. God's freedom to be who he is and to act as he will means spontaneity and involves us in flexible and adaptable patterns of evangelistic outreach.

In this connection, we must say a word about those who would like to have a firm structure in hand to assist them in their evangelistic task. I have learned that there are two big reasons why many professed Christians do not share their witness. They feel inadequate either because they think their own Christian experiences or lives are less than they should be, or they feel that they do not know the right words to say. In connection with our own sense of unworthiness, we can say that we never will reach the point where we can be satisfied and complacent about ourselves. But, even so, our witness is like a signpost that points beyond ourselves to the reality that is our goal and destination—our new life in Christ.

As helpful as it might be to have "a plan of salvation" in hand, we must conclude there is no evidence at all that Jesus had such a plan or method in his mind as he talked to Nicodemus or to the woman of Samaria, to the rich young ruler, to Zacchaeus, or to many others. He began where they were. We find that he did speak to Nicodemus about "being born again," but Jesus never used that same language again in talking with others in face-to-face conversation. Yet the woman of Samaria appears to have needed the new birth as much as Nicodemus! But, Jesus refused to canonize any one set of words or any one systematic or mechanical plan of approach, which he had to develop step-by-step as a part of his effective approach to other people. If you have not felt comfortable with memorizing a single plan of action as your evangelism style, it may well be because you have already caught the method of Jesus' evangelistic style. He had no single plan which he used. As a result, he was not less effective, but more effective.

We are not attacking those who do person-to-person evangelism with a method and a plan in mind. We all profit from having structures, and we can use temporary scaffolds to good advantage. Later, I shall be offering a suggested structure and methodology which will make use of the New Testament in Today's English Version. But, in using structures and methods, we must not be led to mistake the method for the message. Our maps are not the same as the territory they depict; and, although a map is a helpful instrument in preparing us for our journey, it is not the journey itself. Our evangelistic methods and plans must be treated like maps. And they must reflect accurately the diversity of situations and personal needs, providing alternate routes in our approach to other people.

In a "Peanuts" cartoon, Lucy is in her psychiatrist's booth, and Charlie Brown has come up to see her. Looking up into the sky, Charlie says: "See that plane up there." And, then, not waiting for Lucy to respond, Charlie continues, "It's filled with people who are all going someplace. That's what I'd like to do, go off someplace and start a new life." Buried in the hearts of many people there is a similar feeling, often recognized and unspoken.

Effective person-to-person witnessing will see us developing a double-edged kind of sensitivity. We shall be alert to the guidance of God's own Spirit, which brings us his promised help. But we shall be sensitive also to other people and to their real needs, spoken or unexpressed. As we look and listen and love, we shall meet people where they are. We'll understand where they may be hurting. We will hear their questions and bridge the distance between their fears and our own defensiveness. As good news people, we will respond to them with confirmation, rather than condemnation, and we will express acceptance to conquer alienation. We will seek to love them in the same way in which God's love has reached us unconditionally. Following the example of Jesus, we will refuse to stereotype either our evangelistic approach or our methods. Recognizing the partial nature of our own perceptions (seeing through a glass darkly) and the provisional nature of our knowledge (we know in part bit by bit) and remembering our inability to convert anyone else, we shall give an honest witness and then trust God who, alone, is able to make the seed of witness grow.

8 | Good News— Where We Live

Some of the recurring questions we face in person-to-person evangelism are: "Where is the place where we are to carry out our fundamental task in personal evangelistic witness?" "How can we tell the good news naturally and not artificially?" "How can we find openings where the good news fits and we feel comfortable with both the style and the fit?" "How can we be faithful to our task which is to tell everyone, everywhere, and faithful to the biblical precedent and principles which we see in the unstereotyped methods which Jesus used?" "How can we avoid manipulating other people so we can satisfy their needs and their questions, instead of satisfying our own need to tell or to increase our sense of self-regard as 'faithful'?" To such questions as these, we must now turn briefly and consider some answers. To assist us in expanding our range of perception and understanding, we will be looking at the context of several terms which reoccur in the New Testament. Their meaning can be useful to us as we seek to understand the mandate given to us in personal witness today. We shall discover what the context of our person-to-person witness is meant to be as it is reflected in New Testament perspectives and practices.

The first word gives us a clue about the nature of our witness. *Ekklesia* is the Greek word meaning "assembly," and it was used to describe the assembly of citizens in a Greek city-state. When the Old Testament was translated from the Hebrew language into the Greek language of the Septuagint at Alexandria, *ekklesia* was the word used to describe the people of Israel as a congregation gathered before the

Lord. In fact, the word literally means "to call out of" and suggests a process of selection and choice which forms the assembly of people. In the New Testament, especially in the Pauline letters, *ekklesia* is the word which is used to describe the new Christians who are called into being by Christ and gathered in their congregations as "a church."

This brief background tells us that our person-to-person witness must be done as a part of our self-conscious membership in the church which is the body of Christ in the world. As personal evangelists, we weaken our witness whenever we appear to be functioning as free-lance agents with our own gospel which just recently arrived on the scene with us. In the New Testament, we are told that Christ loved the church and that he builds the church on the confession and faith of each disciple. Although the church has often served to bring discredit on his name, nonetheless, it is possible for us to be personal evangelists today only because of the testimony of earlier generations in church history. Others have labored and we have entered into their labors. In turn, those who may come to believe because of our word of witness cannot be made perfect or complete without us. Our Christian witness is rooted in the reality of the church, and we must be willing to identify ourselves as one of its members. To do otherwise is to divide the body of Christ and to reflect the same sectarian problem which afflicted the church in Corinth. There some felt they belonged to Apollos; others confessed that they belonged to Paul, others to Peter; and the most zealous adherents of bigotry claimed to be related only to Christ.

Our person-to-person witness must be grounded in our life and membership in the church of the living God, which exists as the pillar and ground of truth. Such a membership may appear to be a handicap, especially when the church looks more like part of the disease than the remedy. However, apart from our own relationship and commitment to fellow Christians in our own congregation and in the whole church of Christ around the world, we have no gospel except one which we have devised ourselves. The good news has been entrusted by Christ to his church; so the New Testament asks the person who neglects a vital church relationship, "What have you that you did not receive?" (1 Corinthians 4:7). Our word for evangelism comes from *euanggelion* which means the good news. From this basic sounding board within the Christian fellowship functioning as the body of Christ, we can now examine several additional words which help to amplify our task in personal evangelism. These are words like *marturia, koinonia, didache, leitourgia, diakonia, parresia, paroikia* and *kerugma*.

The Greek word *marturia* gives us our English word "martyr" and means to be a witness. *Leitourgia* gives us our English word "liturgy" and means public worship. *Diakonia* gives us our English word "diaconate" and means to serve. *Kerugma,* from *kerux,* means to serve as a herald, a function much akin to the later task of the town crier at a New England town meeting. *Didache* gives us our English word "didactic" and means teaching. *Koinonia* comes from a word meaning "common" and gives us the word *koine* meaning "common speech" or the vernacular. *Koinonia* is the term used throughout the book of Acts to describe the new fellowship of Christians "in Christ." *Paroikia* is the word from which our English words "parochial" and "parish" are derived, and literally it means "beside the house." If a person lives beside the house, he is not in the house, and hence this word came to describe the life of an exile, or a pilgrim. *Parresia* is made up of two Greek words, *para* meaning "beside" and *rema,* a second term meaning "word" or "speech." Originally, *parresia* referred to the free speech which citizens enjoyed in the Greek city-state public meeting. In the New Testament, the word came to mean confidence and boldness in speaking. This is the word which is used to describe the amazement of the people when they saw the boldness (the *parresia*) of the disciples early in the book of Acts.

All of these terms help to enrich our perspectives about our own person-to-person task of evangelism, announcing the good news. Our membership in the church, we have said, is our main vantage point which offers us the ground and floor of our faith. Our task of personal evangelism is related to our teaching opportunities so that every church school teacher, class officer, and class member must be led to see and to accept the claim of sharing the good news as a part of our teaching-learning ministries. Class agendas can be developed to provide systems of support to keep us growing in our faith while nurturing us in the knowledge of God's truth.

Another setting in the life of the church where our task of personal witness will be found is in the preaching and the public worship of the congregation. If evangelism means telling the good news, so that others may be led to accept Jesus Christ as Lord and Savior and to confess him publicly, the times when the church gathers for preaching, for prayer, and for praise and public worship should provide a setting, week after week, when those who are being added to the church by the Lord can respond in their public affirmation and confession of faith. A perennial harvest can be reaped when the whole congregation is faithful to its evangelistic task. When no one comes at the end of a worship service to profess faith in Christ, this does not necessarily mean that the sermon that Sunday was poor and the worship ineffectual. It may also indicate that the people in the pews have been failing to state their faith in such a winsome way that they, themselves, are bringing others to Christ. There are times when the preacher in the pulpit as a herald may give an uncertain sound. But when personal evangelism is going on among the people of the congregation, the good news of their witness will more than compensate for what the pulpit lacks, just as many a broken play on the football field is saved by other members of the team.

The same point can be emphasized about *koinonia,* the fellowship of the church. Person-to-person witnessing is made powerfully real and contagious when the life of God's people substantiates and validates the reality of grace and gospel. Where we allow the walls and barriers to stand which Christ has already destroyed in his cross, we are guilty of undercutting the impact of our evangelistic message. In the New Testament, people were joined to the Lord before they were able to give a full explanation as to what that relationship meant theologically. They knew that they belonged to Christ and to each other. Out of that mutuality of membership, the meaning of belief took shape and stature and emerged in words, "Behold, how they love one another." That is the testimony about the reality of Christian fellowship which makes personal evangelism most effective because interpersonal relationships are real and not fictitious. If the fellowship of the church is not unrestricted so that there is the glad sound of "whosoever will," we corrupt the gospel; we grieve the Spirit of God; and we invalidate our evangelistic message by our anti-good-news attitudes and methods.

The last three words in our group may be considered together, because they do more than offer us a perspective about our personal witness. These terms suggest the place where person-to-person witnessing is meant to take place. So we must examine these words more closely.

Diakonia, we have already said, refers to the service of God's people. *Parresia,* derived from the voice vote of a Greek citizen, came to mean boldness and confidence. *Paroikia* means to live beside the house, hence, outside the parish. Let's look at how these terms can further illumine our person-to-person evangelistic task.

If evangelism is the good news entrusted to the church by the Spirit of God, evangelism starts there, rooted in both the unity and the diversity of its fellowship: expressed in its *kerugma*—its announcement, its heralding of the good news; its services of public worship—*leitourgia;* and in its body of Christian teaching and learning—

didache. But when evangelism, which starts at the church, stops there, as quite frequently it appears to do, we have betrayed the trust implicit in our stewardship of grace and gospel.

Parresia can remind us that we are citizens of God's kingdom and that we enjoy a free access to the very presence of the King himself. He is the one who gives us our full rights, not only as his subjects, but as his adopted children. Our boldness and confidence stem from our standing before him, together with the task assigned by his own hands. We are meant to function as his envoys, ambassadors in his behalf, sent into the world to represent him and to speak and act on his behalf in the same way and with the same authority with which Christ, our elder brother, was sent into the world. We are to be, as Paul reminded the Christians in Philippi, "a colony of heaven" (Philippians 3:20, Moffatt), planted in the midst of temporal history, even as Philippi was itself a colony of Rome planted in Asia Minor. Our task is to colonize the earth and thereby extend the blessings of God's kingdom to the far ends of the world. *Parresia* tells us that, as Christians, we are given courage and boldness which more than matches the terms of our ambassadorial office and functions.

I remember Lord Carradon describing the ceaseless exchange of cables going back and forth between him, as the United Kingdom's ambassador to the United Nations, and his home office in London during the Suez crisis in the Middle East. At the UN Center in New York City, miles away from his nation's government, Lord Carradon had to keep in touch and in tune with the head of state, but his assignment was at his post of duty. So God's envoys keep open lines for updated instructions, but for person-to-person witness we are to be at the post of duty in the real life of the world where we are sent by the commission of Christ.

This perception about our evangelistic task is supported by understanding the thrust of the term *diakonia*—the ministry of service to be performed by the good news people of God. Our pattern to interpret *diakonia* is derived from the servant ministry of Jesus. In the body of his incarnation, he came to reconcile the world from its estrangement to God. He came to redeem the world from its bondage to sin, to death, and to despair. He came to renew the world as he worked in cooperation with the creative intent of God to complete and fulfill the original purpose of God in creation. The ministry of Jesus is a service directed both to the cosmos and to the covenant community of Israel. Beyond that, the ministry of Jesus is directed ultimately to the nations of the world. People of every tongue and of every nation are destined to sit together at his table.

The exaltation of Jesus after his resurrection is marked by the gift of the Holy Spirit. The Spirit is sent in the name of Christ to form the church as his body in the world. The ministry of the church is not to itself or to its members. Instead, the commandment of Jesus for the church in its Great Commission is, literally, "Disciple the nations." His people, without exception, are to be his witnesses to everyone, everywhere. The church lives to serve the world because the servant is not above his master. Jesus explains to his disciples that "the field is the world." The good seed are to be the children of the kingdom. The church is the diaconate of the world. The place where our person-to-person witnessing is to occur is not in religious enclaves but wherever we are in the world. Our jobs, our secular relationships and memberships, in the factory, in the school, in business, on the farm, at our workbench, in the office, in our homes, in our neighborhoods—the field is the world. We are members of God's evangelistic diaconate, dispersed into those settings which are a natural part of our personal lives. And our personal lives (we have already noted) mean, not only our inward, private, interior existence, but also our public and social dimensions of being and membership which must be involved, as well, in our person-to-person task.

The last word, *paroikia,* reminds us that the living God of the universe does not dwell in temples made by human hands. The heaven of heavens cannot contain him. To be part of the *paroikia* means to be living outside the house. Its first meaning in the New Testament speaks of the fact that Christians are pilgrims in this passing age. We are to have our goal in sight ahead of us. We can be sure that we have authority and instructions standing behind us to empower us and give us boldness and confidence, but our post of duty is "outside the house" in the world. As we have seen already, that world includes its people, its reality in nature, and its institutional settings and organizational structures in the public realm. We are not to be *of* the world; that is true, because our citizenship is in heaven, but as good news people, we are to be *in* the world, sharing its pain and lifting its need into the reconciling action of God's love.

When we get these perspectives straight in our heads and these perceptions clear in our vision, we shall be ready to accept our task to be good news people marked by the distinctive evangelistic life style witnessing to everyone, everywhere, with good news for the whole world and the whole person. Not many of us may be called upon to be witnesses in the sense of martyrdom, but our witness must mean that we testify about God's salvation, which in the Greek New Testament meant wholeness. Sight for the blind, hearing for the deaf, healing for the sickness of mind and spirit which often afflicts our bodies as well, wholeness for our brokenness, a new identity and integrity in Christ—this is the message of God's salvation. Salvation includes membership in a new community of faith and love, with its interdependent mutuality which replaces our isolated independence and life of selfishness. And God's salvation entrusts to us a new stewardship of caring love for the world to replace our indolence and neglect which maims the world and cripples our own humanity.

These are the evangelistic perspectives and perceptions which we must take to heart from the biblical context if we are to qualify in our person-to-person witness today. Our witness begins in the church and in the *euanggelion*—the good news entrusted to all of its people in the fellowship of Christ. But, evangelism must complete itself in the life of the world where we spend the major part of our lives and time fulfilling our vocational stewardship commitment as Christians.

Some time ago, one university created a new faculty post to be known as a professorship in human ecology. This meant that doctors, instead of studying us as patients in their consulting rooms and on their operating tables and being concerned only with disease, would begin to focus concern on the reality of health and the meaning of our lives as human beings. The professorship of human ecology was established to study our lives in the context of those places where we live in the midst of our habits and customs of our routine existence. One could conclude that the ecology of personal evangelism is in the context of our human environment amid the problems and the tensions of our existence in the world. If one wonders where we gain the inspiration for such a perception, we do not need to look beyond the ministry of Jesus. The main context of his relationships to the world were established outside the official sanctions and religious duties of the sacred precincts of the temple. And since his exaltation, the New Testament witnesses to his continuing mission. In the book of Revelation and in the book of Hebrews, he is seen at the right hand of the throne of the majesty on high. But, in the book of Colossians, he is also seen at work in the processes of human history by his continuing Spirit. And in the book of Ephesians, he is seen embodied in the life of the new humanity. He continues to be, as John said he was, the light which lightens every person coming into the world.

9 | Deciding for the Good News

As this chapter begins, it may be helpful for us to look back over the way we have come and to attempt a brief summary. We have been saying that God has acted in Jesus Christ to open a new way of access for everyone, everywhere, whereby we can be saved. God's promise has been fulfilled in the event of Christ. We have good news which is greater than the bad news of the sin of our misbegotten world and its brokenness and alienation. The good news is celebrated in Christmas, Calvary, Easter, Ascension, Pentecost, and the promised Parousia. The gospel means good news for the planet Earth and for the whole person.

Through our acceptance of the good news, we are related both to the reality of God's saving love as his adopted sons and daughters and to the reality of nature as faithful stewards, as well as to the whole human family as brothers and sisters. God's grace puts us all together as persons in our private, social, and public dimensions of being. The recovery of our identity in Christ assures us of a new integrity, so that we do not need to use up our psychic energy any longer, either in hiding or pretending. Set free to become what we are meant to be in Christ, we are enabled to accept our membership in the human family and to contribute to its solidarity by a life of interdependence, "members one of another." Out of that position of mutual support, we are encouraged to accept the reality of Christ's lordship over our lives and over the world. Acknowledging that we have another King, we recognize his right to rule and overrule and to requisition our time, our energy, and our influence to be used in a new way. We accept

God's call to care for, to conserve, and to build up the resources of the earth as a heritage for unborn generations.

This stewardship of compassion, of concern, and of faithfulness is what some have come to describe as "eco-justice." Simply put, that term means we are led to care for the earth as a part of God's creation and that we care for other members of the human family as those for whom Christ died and rose again, so that they may share with us in the bounty of God's goodness which includes material as well as spiritual blessings.

We have come to see that God's salvation fulfills the potential of our life, including the social and public dimensions of our human existence, as well as the private, interior aspects of our person. To invite another person to give himself to Jesus Christ and to accept his saving help turns out to be a decision with unlimited consequences. To decide for Christ means a new wholeness which leaves nothing outside of his concern and control. Nowhere is this more evident than in the missionary outreach of the Christian church. In giving Christ to other nations of the world, some may have thought that they were bestowing a spiritual benefit only for the private person. But, in Third-World nations where colonialization had contributed to their slow rate of political, social, and economic development, decisions for Christ contributed significantly to upset colonialism because, as Savior, he sets his people free. Freedom meant to be free, not only from spiritual tyranny, but also from other tyrannies that had become oppressive in the public realm of politics and in the social realm of society. A decision for Christ in the Third World meant radical change but without revolution. A decision for Christ meant literacy and knowledge. To decide for Christ meant medicine and healing. To decide for Christ meant agricultural mission and a new way to husband the earth. A "yes" for Christ meant a "no" to polygamy where women had been regarded as chattel property. A "yes" for Christ meant a "no" to exposure of unwanted children as each person gained a new dignity and value. A "yes" for Christ meant a "no" to social caste systems and their taboos. A "yes" for Christ meant a "no" to religious fetishism and voodoo. A "yes" for Christ meant a "yes" to social hygiene, a "yes" to life, a "yes" to the world of nature as a part of God's creation, a "yes" to the whole lordship of Christ over all of life and its interdependent existence.

To understand what a decision for Christ has meant in the missionary world of younger churches is to raise the question among Christians in America whether we do not seriously misrepresent the good news in our person-to-person witness when we ask people to

make only a marginal and casual commitment for Christ. His salvation is meant to do more than bring about superficial and surface changes in our style of life. Hence, to assist us in our evangelistic task, we need to be able to explain what it means when we ask a person to decide for the good news. We must be able to answer the question of what is involved when we give the invitation to follow Jesus Christ all the days of our lives and to profess him publicly as Lord and Savior. Our situation may be like that state which several years ago had two different men occupying the governor's office, each one claiming to be governor of the state. State agencies and the people in them had to make a decision as to who would be governor and have the right to command their loyalty and to exercise leadership and authority commensurate with the office. So, we must make a choice between Christ and Caesar, between Christ as King and the false rulers of the universe. As Christ warns us, it is not enough to call him Lord with our lips unless his lordship is embodied in our lives. As we begin to manifest the marks of an evangelistic life style, these characteristics will serve as criteria, helping to deepen our common awareness of what a "yes" to Christ is destined to mean.

1. Deciding for the good news means a decision of faith in the person of Jesus Christ as Lord and Savior. In the confession of the apostolic church, there is not even a second name "by which we must be saved" (Acts 4:12). Obviously, this passage does not refer to the English name for Jesus. Otherwise, millions of people who know his name in other languages would still be lost. No single name by which Jesus is known is able to describe the fullness which resides in him. As the Savior of the whole world, he is greater than all his names and titles from every speech and language. What the Bible means, therefore, when it refers to the name of Jesus is his essential nature and character as a person and his meaning and adequacy for us and for the world as our Savior.

A decision for the good news means to accept all that God promises which comes into focus in the life and work of Christ. We know Jesus as able to save all who come to God by him. We know him as able to keep us from stumbling and to steady our steps. We come to know him as able to do exceeding abundantly above all that we ask or think. We know him as able to keep what we entrust to him and as able to subdue all things unto himself in line with his eternal purpose. A decision for the good news is a decision of faith in the adequacy of Christ as Savior; it means a decision to follow him as leader and guide; it means a decision for fellowship with him as friend and companion; it means a decision to offer him our fealty and service as Lord. All of this becomes clear in terms of what he claims to be and what we discover him to be in our continuing pilgrimage and experience.

2. A decision for the good news is a decision for both process and progress. To become a Christian is to believe on the name of Jesus Christ and to belong to him and to the people he gathers for mission, fellowship, and service. To be a Christian is a decision to become *more* than, as well as *other* than, what we are. These are important facts because progress and process both involve personal growth and change, and they suggest a final destination as the end product of present directions.

Christian experience represents a break with the past and a change in direction in one's personal goals. If the Christian life begins with our decision—our deciding for Christ and the good news—the

Christian life continues as experience because of additional commitments and decisions we make and the deeper conversions we experience. We may recall Jesus saying to Simon Peter who had been a disciple for several years, "When you have turned again, strengthen your brethren" (Luke 22:32). Simon Peter is already a new creation in Christ, but his first decision was to a process which brought about additional changes (conversions!) in his life.

What appears to happen in personal conversion is that the self-conscious areas of life are changed, but the subconscious areas, buried deep within us, await their outward transformation as they, too, may be changed in the renewing of our minds. This is why, at the end of his life, the apostle Paul confessed, "I have not yet attained; it is not as though I am already perfect [complete]. But I follow after, I pursue the goal to reach the prize of ultimate likeness to Christ." (See Philippians 3:12-13.) Paul's decision for Christ, involved in his Damascus Road experience, was to a process involving progress for the rest of his life. He called it "walking in the Lord." The apostle Peter in his letter called it a pilgrimage. It starts with the first step of faith, but it is never finished within time. To speak descriptively of God's salvation, one should say "I have been saved, I am being saved, I will be saved." Because Christ himself is the same yesterday, today, and forever, and he lives forever as the Author of an eternal salvation, our decision must include all the tenses of time—past, present, and future. To decide for the good news is to give all we know about ourselves to all that we know about Jesus Christ. Because our self-conscious awareness and knowledge will increase in self-discovery, and because our knowledge of Christ will grow, any single decision for Christ must be to a process and to its inherent sense of progress.

A. H. Maslow has worked out a hierarchy of human needs which he sees as descriptive of the motivational factors in a person's decisions. He suggests that as basic physiological needs are met and satisfied (never 100 percent satisfied), we are enabled to move to a higher level of motivational need and choice. After safety and security needs are met, we seek to fulfill ourselves by meeting growth needs, such as meaningfulness, order, beauty, and goodness. Maslow says that some people spend all their lives, like the rich fool in Jesus' parable, seeking ways to satisfy their physiological needs and their safety and security needs. But the growth needs impinge upon a person, like the atmosphere itself upon the body, with equal pressure at all points on our existence.[1]

[1] Quoted in Frank Goble, *The Third Force* (New York: Grossman Publishers, 1970), pp. 36-51.

Keith Miller has reminded us that many people have gotten converted at the level of safety and security needs.[2] One can think of all the gospel songs with such a theme: "Safe in the Arms of Jesus," "A Shelter in the Time of Storm," "A Mighty Fortress Is Our God." If we misunderstand the nature of our Christian experience in conversion, we will be tempted to hunker down and hide somewhere in church behind the original bunker where Jesus met us. Only as we help each other to see that a decision for Christ must be a decision for progress and process will we be able to understand the full work of divine grace in the transformation of our whole life. Christ came not only to satisfy our need for safety and security, but also he came to satisfy all of the hungers of our being for growth and meaning. If we do not see this in our person-to-person witnessing, a tragic result will be that people are converted, not to walk in the light, but to mark time as they remain where they were, as they were. Unfortunately, the light moves on beyond our repeated dress parades to where God's action is!

3. A decision for the good news which involves a personal decision of faith in Christ as Lord and Savior and which is a decision for process and progress becomes also a decision which engages the whole person. Many people first find Christ in the private sector of their being because that may be the place where they are experiencing their deepest sense of estrangement and alienation and need. Christ meets them at the point of their felt needs. But, if only the private part of our personal existence is saved, vast domains are left outside the controlling power of Christ's lordship!

"D-Day" in Normandy was a launching date when the Allied Forces landed in France, seeking to regain control of western Europe from the tyranny of the Nazi occupation. But, although the landing beachheads were crucially important in that mission, the cities, the capitals of nations, and the cultural and controlling centers of Europe had to be set free so their powers in government and society could support the life of personal freedom. The conversion of the private person is like the beachhead where Christ first occupies our being. But if he does not also occupy and control the social and public dimensions of our personhood, the major part of our daily life where many important decisions are made and lived out will be "outside" of Christ instead of being "in Christ." That's why our person-to-person witness must illumine the truth that our decision for Christ must include the *whole* person. Christians who spend five minutes a day

[2] Keith Miller, *The Becomers* (Waco, Tex.: Word, Inc., 1973), pp. 93-99.

thinking about Christ in their private temples of faith and sixteen hours a day thinking and working in the social and public realms of their personal existence will discover that these other parts of their being are about 192 times more real. Our conversion, therefore, must include the whole person. Otherwise, most of our life will go on in its own direction with its own momentum almost exclusively unrelated to the scant few hours we may spend in private religious devotion at home or in church. God's aim is to establish his control in all of our being. He wants all the keys to all the rooms in our nature.

4. In our person-to-person witness, we must also remember that a decision for the good news means a decision and commitment to God's people. To be added to the Lord means to be added to his church which serves as the body of his Presence and ministry in the world. To read 1 Corinthians 12 and Romans 12 and the book of Ephesians is to gain a new understanding that he who says he loves God whom he has not seen, but does not love his brother whom he does see, is making a false claim and assertion; the truth is not in him. Christian community exists to confirm each member in it and to complete our partial perspectives and understanding. Christian community exists to offer us the security of understanding love and support while correcting us by its standards and expectations. Christian community exists to help us name our experience, to support us in its believing fellowship and to enable us to run the risk for obedience to God's call and claim in ministry and service. No Christian can think of himself as independent of either Christ or of his body. To decide for the good news is to choose, like Moses, to suffer affliction with the people of God rather than to enjoy the pleasures of sin for a season. Our decision means a mutual membership in a life of Christian solidarity not separate from but united with others.

5. In person-to-person witness, we can help others to see that a decision for the good news means a decision and a commitment to God's purposes revealed in Jesus Christ. Christ came on the Father's mission. It was his steady aim to do the Father's will. He encourages his disciples to pray that the will of the Father might be done on earth as it is done in heaven. To discover what God is up to in his concern and love for the world, we could turn to the last pictures of the world that is yet to come. In Revelation, chapters 21 and 22 help to fill out the content in our understanding. We discover new heavens and a new earth; we see a city without walls, a city without a temple because the Lord God Almighty and the Lamb are the temple thereof. We see a city without night, where no shadows lurk to create fear. We see a city without pain, without tears, without injustice, and without death.

A person's decision for Christ means a willingness to offer life in its totality as an instrument in behalf of the eternal purposes of God. We give ourselves to accept the stewardship of service, and we accept Jesus' invitation to join him as fellow workers. We do not bring his kingdom with us, it is true, but where the King comes and where the King is, he brings his kingdom with him. A decision for Christ, the King, is a decision to seek first his kingdom and to announce the good news that his kingdom is at hand, even though it is not yet fully realized. To decide for Christ is to devote one's life in a new way, to relate to his world in a new way, to serve its future long-term needs in a new way. A decision for Christ is a decision to do good to all men, especially those in the household of faith.

6. Last of all, a decision for Christ and the good news means a covenant decision to become a good news person with an evangelistic life style, engaging us in personal witness wherever we live and work. In love, we will seek to engage our neighbor in a meeting of meaning. We shall seek to bridge our differences and alienation, our fears, our caution, and our timidity so we can more effectively share the good news of Christ. Our sense of urgency will be increased because of what others are missing outside of Christ. But our sense of urgency will be enhanced because the love of Christ leaves us no choice but to share the burden of love's concern for all who, in Christ's redemptive reach, are meant to be our next of kin.

I have a friend who was a working colleague for some years. Quiet, modest, and unassuming, Henry Bondurant left an indelible imprint wherever he lived. I remember his telling about a tragedy which had overtaken him and his family. Late one night, his youngest son was driving home. His car went out of control, flipped over, and caught fire. Others happened on the scene of the accident, but, as one man reported, the flames enveloping the burning car seemed too intense to attempt a rescue even though they thought they could hear the youth calling for help. In relating that incident, Henry said, "I can understand how all the spectators felt, but I think if I had been there, I would have tried to get him out." The difference is the intensity of love. A bystander, moved by a sense of duty, might have tried some act of heroism, although none did. But a father acts not out of a sense of duty, but because he loves and cares for his own. Thus it has always been with God. So may it become for all of us.

Our task is clear. Our resources are greater than all the needs and their demand. Enabled and empowered by God, we are meant to share a vital and contagious witness.

10 | The Good News in Action

We have examined several biblical models and discovered how sensitive Jesus was in his person-to-person witness. He refused to stereotype people or to impoverish the methods of approach and relationship to others. He revealed that God is not limited in the access which he has to us. We have come to understand that we must not mechanize or canonize our own means or methods, but, like Jesus, we must use a dialogical approach and establish a language of relationship which can be more important than the words we may be led to say. Now, to assist you in moving toward the development of your own style of Christian witness, I am suggesting an approach especially designed for those who may feel both uncomfortable and defenseless without a structured guide. (See Appendix A.) No scaffold is meant to be regarded as a part of the permanent structure. At the same time, a scaffold may be a necessary instrument to achieve a certain desired end in relationship to the building itself. If we can remember that it is the Spirit of God who is the best evangelist, we can make ourselves available to his guidance and help to develop our own style of witness, which will be most authentically real. Just as no one can make your own decisions for you by proxy, no one can take your place in sharing your own witness. As the parents of the blind man said to those interrogating them as to how their son had been healed, "He is of age, ask him" (John 9:1-23). To come of age as a Christian is to be able in our own way to give our own witness and testimony helpfully, persuasively, yet honestly.

To start with, take two copies of the paperback, *Good News for*

Modern Man.[1] In these copies, you can underline those verses of Scripture which help to illustrate the essential parts which you deem vital to your own Christian witness. After you have made an appointment to meet, you can present your friend with the second copy and ask him or her to follow you in your conversation as you explain the meaning of your faith and share your witness for Christ. It will prove helpful if you underline the Scriptures on each page to

which you will be referring. Then at the bottom of each page where a Scripture reference is noted, write down the page number of the next reference; for example, "please turn to page 22." (Be sure to check the references and page numbers in the edition which you have.) Here's how a suggested conversation for witness might develop.

As your conversation begins, you will want to be a good listener. It is important for you to discover not only who the person is, but also where that person is. He or she may have made a commitment for Christ as a youth. You need to know not only what the person is currently thinking, but also how he or she is feeling. You need to know what is that person's self-image and the questions that he or she has. Your witness will be effective and helpful in the measure that you are able to relate to the other as a real person that the gospel of Jesus does not appear to be like a can of peaches, which we open and serve indiscriminately to everyone. In establishing a dialogical approach of conversation, you will have made yourself accessible, available,

[1] *Good News for Modern Man* (New York: American Bible Society, 1971).

affirmatively accepting and responsive so that the person's situation has opportunity to emerge, together with his sense of need. (See Appendix B.) You will keep in mind Maslow's hierarchy of needs described in the previous chapter, and you will be seeking ways in which your conversation can illustrate how Christ satisfies these deep-rooted spiritual and emotional needs in each of us as persons. Such needs include our need to belong, to be valued and esteemed by others, to be better than we are, to be growing toward wholeness; our need to love and to serve and to be loved; our need for understanding; our need for meaning and purpose in our life and work; and our need for a faith stronger than our fears and a hope replacing doubt and despair.

Your person-to-person witness could then follow an approach similar to the following:

The good news for you is that God loves you unconditionally. Please turn to page 233 in the *Good News for Modern Man* New Testament. As we read John 3:16-17, underlined on that page, we will discover that God's love for the world led him to give his own Son, not as our judge, but as our Savior. This same idea is underscored on page 376 in the text underlined in Romans 5:6-11. This passage illustrates how much God loves us! While we were still sinners, Christ died for us, so that we could become one of God's friends!

Please turn to page 466. Chapter 2 of Paul's Letter to the Ephesians describes not just the human predicament and problem, but the initiative which characterizes God's loving action in our behalf. The entire section which starts at the top of page 466 and is completed on page 467 is a mirror which shows us our old face outside of Christ and our new face as a Christian. It may be helpful for us to analyze the main points of the chapter.

We discover that without Christ or outside of Christ we are dead spiritually. God surrounds our life with providential mercies and care, but we are blind to his presence, deaf to his voice. We are like a runaway child who never writes home and who returns letters from home unopened and unread.

Verse 2 tells us that we follow a leader, but it turns out to be the wrong leader. The false rulers of this age controlling our lives only deepen our sense of rebellion and our distance from God.

Verse 3 points out that instead of experiencing God's presence as love, we experience the reality of God outside of Christ as wrath.

Our sense of alienation produces guilt, and guilt makes us misbehave in order to be punished or to punish ourselves. However, punishment does not make us feel less guilty; it makes us feel more guilty. We are like a person mired in quicksand. Struggling to get free, the victim feels a hope of getting out of the predicament; yet the struggle only complicates and deepens the plight.

Verses 4-7 tell us how God has responded to us and to our human need. His response is because of his own rich mercy and great love. God acts characteristically with mercy and love because those are essential aspects of his divine character. We also discover that God has acted while we were spiritually dead. Helpless and impotent, we could not forgive ourselves nor could we save ourselves. But God has brought us to life in Christ. The force of this allusion to the resurrection of Jesus tells us that the same power which God used to raise Jesus Christ from the dead is available and at work in our situation to shatter our bondage and to deliver us from our old servitude. With Christ's exaltation we are raised to share the newness of his life and situation. No longer slaves, we are now God's free people and God has given us our full rights as citizens in his kingdom and, more than that, as children in his own household.

Verses 8-10 emphasize that all of this is of God's own doing. His grace is given to us even though we do not deserve it. God never stops loving us despite our willfulness and waywardness. His love turns out to be unconditional. We are saved by grace through faith and this is not of our own doing; it is the gift of God. If God's initiative for our salvation is prompted by the nature of his own love and grace, we are asked to accept personally and to make a personal response which is appropriate to God's action. He offers us his gift of life in Christ. God has said "yes" to us, and his affirming "yes" is the means for our achieving all that we have been missing outside of Christ. But God's "yes" awaits our "yes," our confirming choice, our commitment of faith, our own decision. Our "yes" instead of our "no" is needed as our response to God's unconditional acceptance of us in the love of Christ. Verse 10 reminds us that God has a place for us to fill in creative partnership with him. But our "yes" is needed to complete the covenant which he has made in our behalf.

Verses 11-12 outline for us what the awful consequences of a continued "no" to God's love leads to. We are apart from Christ; we are aliens; we don't feel as if we belong to the people of God; we are rootless and anonymous; we are without an identity and integrity of our own; we have no share in the covenants of promise, life is without meaning and foundation, we live without hope, without a sense of God, without a future. The result is an awful sense of existential despair and anxious dread. Our alienation from God and from our neighbor, from nature and from ourselves is a living death. This is the plight and predicament of modern man and reflects the same plight and predicament of persons in every century wherever people have attempted to live outside of the redemptive life in Jesus Christ. But now the balance of the chapter reveals how God's initiative in love has taken notice of our nature and our need and has acted to provide his salvation, radically altering our human situation.

Verses 13-22 provide us with a summary of what God has done for the world and for us as persons in Jesus Christ. Verse 13 signifies that he has united us in Christ. We are no longer far away; we are brought near by the death of Jesus. Verses 14-15 assure us that we have peace because animosity and alienation have been overcome and we are now joined together as one people. Christ has broken down the walls of division that kept us apart and has made us one in himself. Salvation not only enables us to be made whole as persons in the private and the social and the public dimensions of our existence in a new integration of self, but salvation also creates Christian community with its sense of mutuality and interdependence. Beyond that, God's salvation and redemption is linked to his concern for the world so that it, too, may be saved from its thralldom of decay. We become instruments of God's purpose in behalf of its cosmic range and intent as we accept the stewardship entrusted in our new relationship, as fellow workers with Christ.

Verses 16-18 remind us that it is the death of Christ on the cross (symbolizing the love of God) which has destroyed the enmity existing in our old situation. We are given a new access to God.

Verses 19-22 tell how our situation is radically changed by Christ's action. We are no more aliens, no longer exiles or strangers, but now we are fellow citizens. We are full members of

God's family. We are a vital part of Christ's purpose, continuing in the world where we form a temple of his own Spirit and presence.

The total impact of this chapter is unmistakably good news for everyone, everywhere, to replace the bad news of our human predicament and plight. God has effectively dealt with the predicament of our divided self. His love has already acted in our behalf to make up the long-term deficits in our personal situation. That situation is accurately perceived and described without illusion many places in the Bible. But our situation is also described by contemporary playwrights and dramatists and by authors and artists. Many of these persons may not be professed Christians, but they are able to tell us what the human predicament is like in varying tones and texts and colors. So, we read about our situation as "strangeness," as "estrangement," as "alienation," as "anxious dread," as "sickness unto death," as "meaninglessness and despair," as "hostility and aggression," as "anonymity," and "a crisis of identity and integrity," as a "self disesteemed and disowned," and as "a self not OK." From many sectors and quarters of human experience we discover that there is a huge deficit which is the bad news of our situation. Our form and features are represented in contemporary art as fragmented, lacerated, distorted, and disordered. Many are the pictures and diverse are the terms, but they all speak to us of a person living without God and without hope in the world. And somewhere in that collage we see our own features.

But the good news for each of us is that God's love separates us from the crowd, speaks our own name, and makes us whole again. He unites us to himself, forms a new community of faith and love and hope which becomes the instrument of his continuing concerns and purposes for the world. We can further spell out the meaning of the good news in terms of God's unconditional love and action in Jesus Christ as follows:

1. The good news for us means life instead of death. Please turn to page 239. The text underscored in John 5:24 testifies that our belief in Christ means eternal life instead of judgment as one who has already passed from death to life. This same truth is underscored on page 377 in the text underlined in Romans 5:21. But in each case, it is clear that we must be willing to make a personal choice—to say our "yes" to God's gift in Jesus Christ. Our "yes," represented in our decision of faith, turns out to be a monumental "yes" to life and a "no" to the powers of sin and death. That confidence emerges unshakable in a

passage like that found on page 528 in Hebrews 2:14-16. We are informed of the staggering fact that Christ has already destroyed the power of the Devil who had the controlling power of death with its lifelong dread and fear.

2. But the good news for us also means forgiveness for our sin and our guilt. On that same page, 528, the passage underlined in Hebrews 2:17-18 points out that Jesus functions as a sympathetic high priest in order that our sins may find their full forgiveness in Him. Please turn now to page 541. The passage underlined in Hebrews 10:12-18 tells us that Christ has acted once and for all to put away sin by the sacrifice of himself. We have the pledge and the promise of God in Hebrews 10:17, "I will not remember their sins and wicked deeds any longer." Forgiveness is possible in Christ! Please turn also to page 575. The verses underscored in 1 John 2:1-2 provide an open invitation that if we confess our sins, God is faithful and just to forgive us and to cleanse us from every evil. We can conclude that either our sin has been confessed and therefore has been forgiven, or it is still in us as sin. Our "yes" to Christ is a "yes" to accept the reality of forgiveness.

3. The good news for us also means a recovery of personal identity and integrity to replace our sense of anonymity and namelessness. If you will turn to page 438, you will find the passage underscored is 2 Corinthians 5:17, which assures us that our "yes" to the good news can mean the start of a brand-new life in Christ. The old is gone; the new has come. In the same way, the incident recorded on pages 203-204 reveals how our personal response to Christ brings about significant changes which are expressed in life (Luke 19:1-10). When salvation comes to your house, you have a new wholeness, a new self-respect which leads to a new beginning and to a new process in life.

4. The good news for us means adoption into God's family as full members and makes for a new sense of community. God's acceptance in adoption replaces our sense of alienation. If you will turn to page 382, the passage in Romans 8:14-17, underlined, speaks of God's action to declare us his own children. His acceptance accepted by us leads to a new self-acceptance, the acceptance of others, both in the household of faith and in the entire human family. From our life of selfish isolation, insulated from others, we recover the interdependence and mutuality of family life intended by God in his first creation. This same point is made on page 227 in John 1:12, which is underlined. Those who receive Christ gain their adoption papers and their full rights as God's children. Another passage confirming us in this same relationship is described on page 458 where Galatians 4:4-7 is underlined. God gives us his own Spirit to

establish our full confidence that we are his children. Now we can be sure that we belong. We have unbroken ties of affiliation which overrule and conquer our earlier estrangement and homesickness. We are no longer slaves, but children, and since we are his children, God gives us all that he has so that we may live out of his fullness and exercise a mutual care and regard for others.

5. The good news for us means a new mission in life in partnership with Christ. Please turn to 237, where John 4:34 is underlined. You will discover that our "yes" to Jesus Christ means that we are united with him in the unfinished task of doing the will of his heavenly Father and completing his work on the earth. God's original concern is brought into focus in the life and mission of Jesus. As we are yoked with him, we become stewards of God's truth, but we act also as God's stewards in relationship to his redemptive purposes for the earth, for nature, for human society, and for the nations of the whole world. Like Jesus in the body of his incarnation, we, too, are meant to be instruments of God's love and redemption in our own time. If you will turn to pages 382-383, you will see in the passage underlined, Romans 8:21-23, that God has given us an undefeatable hope that creation itself will be set free from its slavery to decay. Its present pain, like the pain of childbirth, will lead to a new life.

6. The good news for us is that everywhere and always we are assured of Christ's saving presence and help. If you will turn to page 83, we have the promise underlined in Matthew 28:20, "Remember, I will be with you always." His inseparable presence means the gift of his peace and of his power. On page 270 (John 14:27), Jesus tells us, in effect, do not be upset and do not be afraid; my peace I give unto you. On page 482, Philippians 4:7, the apostle Paul testifies that he has received in his own experience the gift of peace which has steadied his steps and has carried him through the most upsetting and distressing circumstances of life. We discover that God's help is not distant to us but is near at hand. In the book of Hebrews, several passages illustrate that hope. On page 531, Hebrews 4:14-16 assures us that Jesus has sympathy and understanding with our weaknesses and needs because of his own humanity. Turning to him, we find mercy and grace to help us just when we need it. On page 536 (Hebrews 7:23-25), we are informed that because Jesus lives forever, his work does not pass on to anyone else. Therefore, he is able now and always to save those who come to God through him because he lives forever to speak in their behalf and to help them. In the last chapter of Hebrews on page 549 (Hebrews 13:5-6), we have the confident conviction which emerges, "The Lord is my helper, I will not be afraid." God is a

very present help in time of trouble so that we are made adequate for every test, for every trust, and for every task which is a part of our life and work. And God's help is not only outside of us but is granted to us at the very center of our own being, as the place where a person loves and hates, thinks and reasons, values and chooses and decides. As the apostle Paul testified on page 483 (Philippians 4:12-13), "I have learned this secret. . . . I have the strength to face all conditions by the power that Christ gives me."

The good news is summarized in that Christ gives us a new relationship to God. We enjoy his forgiveness and reconciliation. We know that God has acted so we can be sure of his accepting, confirming, and transforming love. On page 376 (Romans 5:1-2), we are assured that because "we have been put right with God through faith, we have peace with God through our Lord Jesus Christ." God's action in pronouncing us "not guilty"—acquitting us—emphasized on page 383 (Romans 8:33-35) assures us that, since it is God himself who has pronounced us "not guilty," no one else is able to condemn us. No one can upset his verdict, and we shall never be placed in double jeopardy. The good news means adoption into God's family where we are reconciled to him, to others, and to ourselves. Our alienation in the world is overcome also in the cosmic reach of the cross of Christ. This point is underscored on page 486 (Colossians 1:19-20), "Through the Son, then, God decided to bring the whole universe back to himself. God made peace through his Son's death on the cross, and so brought back to himself all things, both on earth and in heaven."

This brief summary of the good news offers us a small glimpse of what shall continue to expand in our own reading of the Bible and its study. But such a beginning can enable us in our person-to-person witness to encourage others to respond with personal faith and to profess that faith publicly in Jesus Christ. Faith includes more than the credibility of other people and other facts. Faith, in the New Testament, is a willingness to trust one's whole self to God's love and action. Many people believe in God's existence, but they have never acted personally to accept God's acceptance of them. We can help these people to understand that faith is, first, a decision to believe the good news, that these truths we have been looking at are true for each of us. Secondly, we can encourage them to know that faith is a personal decision, enabling us to belong to Jesus Christ and to own him as our personal Savior and friend. Thirdly, we can help them understand that faith is a personal decision to become what God intends us to be, a new person in Christ with a new outlook, a new consciousness, and a new commitment to serve as a vital part of God's community of hope and love. This life, embracing an entirely new evangelistic life style as a follower of Jesus Christ, will lead us to a recovery of personal identity and integrity, so that our broken and divided selves can be made whole again. Our decision will enable us to live, not marginally, but in the very center of meaning and purpose supported by the fellowship of believing Christians and by the encouragement of God's own presence. His action in us as the body of Christ empowers us as instruments of his purpose to bear witness to the possibilities of change and transformation which can humanize the world and all the institutions of which we are a part. Our new life in Christ can lead us to accept a new stewardship of influence to help build up the earth and to serve members of our human family with a new sense of justice and compassion. It will be for us the fulfillment of a prophecy offered by Micah:

> "What does the Lord require of you
>   but to do justice, and to love kindness,
>   and to walk humbly with your God?" (Micah 6:8)

A decision of faith is our choice to begin our pilgrimage here and now, to put our hand in God's hand, and to trust him to guide and to lead us day by day all the days of our lives. Our decision is constantly renewed as we give all that we know about ourselves to all that we have come to know about Jesus Christ.

These scriptural passages which are identified here are but a small selection of many similar verses which you can identify for yourself, which can initiate the dialogical process of your evangelistic witness. No single method will ever fully suffice as we may recall from the conversations of Jesus. As we begin to embrace for ourselves our own authentic evangelistic life style, our person-to-person witness will become less arbitrary and mechanical and more dynamic and vital. While we must recognize that methods are limited, we should not refuse to share the good news for lack of a method. "A son who sleeps in harvest," the Bible tells us, "brings shame" (Proverbs 10:5). With God's help, the good news will come alive in us, and we will become good news people bearing the marks of the Lord Jesus wherever we go. For, just as in the New Testament we saw the good news in action, so we shall begin to see in our own churches and in our own generation the good news in action. And that is to see love itself in action!

EPILOGUE

I'll make me a world to fill all this void, and fashion a dome so high in the sky that eagles or spaceships, howe'er deployed, can never out-fly the height of the sky. I'll fill all this space, so empty and vast, as chaos with cosmos, I will replace. Where stars in their courses go winking past, planets in orbit will spin in their place. I'll carve out deep seas from rock and from sand, and fill their sloped saucers from side to side with cloud-seeding rains which, spilled on command, can dower the oceans, each with its tide. I'll pile up the mountains with their high peaks, to tower o'er plains and form distant range, where mixed with their mist, the rainbows can seek to break through the storm and color each flange. I'll make me a world where Love fills all space, where distance is bridged from earth to the sky, from ceiling above to pillars and base, Love's Good News is spilled so men will not die! "Behold!" God says, "I make all things brand new." Good News in action means a people, too!

Appendix A

"Leading" in Person-to-Person Witnessing

In older home visitation evangelistic manuals, a team, calling two-by-two, was encouraged to decide which partner would take the lead in the interview. Most frequently, what that meant was: determine who should open the conversation and take the lead in talking first.

In more recent counseling experience, "leading" is a term which reflects teamwork between the counselor and the client, whereby the counselor's remarks seek to state the next point which the client is ready to accept. This reflects the dialogical mutuality which should also pertain in person-to-person witnessing.

Building blocks in the "leading" process include:

1. *Silence*—our silence when the other person pauses may encourage him to reflect on the last point made and to proceed to a deeper level, because he is ready to do so, without feeling that he is being probed by us.

2. *Acceptance*—an "uhuh" or "yes, I see" may be enough to say that "I understand and accept what you are saying," while such a response does not block the dialogue.

3. *Restatement*—repeating what the other person has said, in his own words, may enable him to reexamine and to modify/clarify his statement without our needing to do so—e.g., we say, "You say that all Christians are hypocrites"—pause—

4. *Clarification*—such leading remarks as "I understand you to say ...."; "Is that right?"; and "Do I read you?" may help clarify his thinking.

5. *Approval*—such approval will generate confidence that he is being heard/understood and can risk further relationship in the dialogue.

6. *Tentative Analysis*—a new approach which we offer on a tentative basis gives the other person the option to accept/modify/or reject the idea.

7. *Interpretation*—"This is what I keep hearing..." "I understand that to mean...." Our interpretation of facts can lead to insight and open up areas of adjustment and growth.

8. *Witness*—sharing meaning from our faith and experience will illumine expressed needs and questions.

9. *Assurance*—validating opinions/reassuring misgivings.

10. *Interrogation*—interrupting the process to question some aspect of our relationship which seems to have gotten off the track. No person-to-person conversation should be closed without leaving relationships *intact*—and the door open for continued interaction.

Appendix B

**A Checklist on Effective Attitudes
in Creating a Helping Relationship***

1. *Can I be what I am?* Carl Rogers calls this honesty, "congruency"—showing ourselves to the other person as genuinely trustworthy, dependable, consistent.

2. *Can I show myself unambiguously?* Interpersonal relationships are blocked by posing, by masking, by defensiveness, or by communicating contradictory messages. To form a helping relationship with another person requires "self-acceptance," a helping relationship to oneself.

3. *Can I manifest positive regard* for the other person? Distance and impersonality can be bridged by warmth, respect, and caring interest.

4. *Can I be strong enough to respect my own feelings* as well as those of the other person? Can I "own" my feelings as separate from his?

5. *Can I be "secure" enough* to permit the other person to exist as he is; can I give him freedom to be—refusing to make him conform to my expectations or to model himself to my desires?

* Adapted from Carl Rogers, *On Becoming a Person* (Boston: Houghton Mifflin Company, 1961), pp. 50-56.

6. *Can I be both empathetic and sympathetic*—allowing myself to step into his world—to see things from where he stands, while withholding the immediate desire to criticize or judge?

7. *Can I accept each part* of the other person's being and behavior— and communicate my unconditional sense of acceptance, without being threatened?

8. *Can I relate to the other person* without allowing my behavior to pose a threat?

9. *Can I withhold the threat* of immediate external evaluation, so I do not act as judge and jury?

10. *Can I meet the other person as one in the process of becoming;* or will I bind him by his past or mine? Rogers quotes Martin Buber's definition of confirming others, "accepting the whole potentiality of the other." Whatever his past, I refuse to treat him as fixed and final!

Our person-to-person evangelistic witness will be most effective when we reflect a helping relationship with its interaction of dialogue and mutuality. After each conversation, we can profit by making process notes—recording how the visit went and noting questions to pursue in our next meeting. In that reflection, it will be helpful to examine this checklist.